Unleashed Influence:
power of servant leadership

Bible Study That Builds Christian Community

SERENDIPITY HOUSE

LIFE CONNECTIONS

Unleashed Influence: Power of Servant Leadership
Student Book

Published by Serendipity House Publishers
Nashville, Tennessee

ISBN: 1-5749-4142-9

Dewey Decimal Classification: 303.3
Subject Headings:
Leadership\Christian Life\Christian Servanthood

To purchase additional copies of this resource or other studies:
ORDER ONLINE at www.SerendipityHouse.com;
VISIT the LifeWay Christian Store nearest you;
WRITE Serendipity House, 117 10th Avenue North, Nashville, TN 37234
FAX (615) 277-8181
PHONE (800) 525-9563

SERENDIPITY® HOUSE
1.800.525.9563
www.SerendipityHouse.com

Printed in the United States of America
10 09 08 07 06 05 04 1 2 3 4 5 6 7 8 9 10

Contents

Core Values

Community: The purpose of this curriculum is to build community within the body of believers around Jesus Christ.

Group Process: To build community, the curriculum must be designed to take a group through a step-by-step process of sharing your story with one another.

Interactive Bible Study: To share your "story," the approach to Scripture in the curriculum needs to be open-ended and right-brained—to "level the playing field" and encourage everyone to share.

Developmental Stages: To provide a healthy program in the life cycle of a group, the curriculum needs to offer courses on three levels of commitment:

(1) **Beginner Level**—low-level entry, high structure, to level the playing field;
(2) **Growth Level**—deeper Bible study, flexible structure, to encourage group accountability;
(3) **Discipleship Level**—in-depth Bible study, open structure, to move the group into high gear.

Target Audiences: To build community throughout the culture of the church, the curriculum needs to be flexible, adaptable, and transferable into the structure of the average church.

Mission: To expand the kingdom of God one person at a time by filling the "empty chair." (We add an extra chair to each group session to remind us of our mission.)

Group Covenant

It is important that your group covenant together, agreeing to live out important group values. Once these values are agreed upon, your group will be on its way to experiencing Christian community. It's very important that your group discuss these values—preferably as you begin this study. The first session would be most appropriate. (Check the rules to which each member of your group agrees.)

- ☐ **Priority:** While you are in this course of study, you give the group meetings priority.
- ☐ **Participation:** Everyone is encouraged to participate and no one dominates.
- ☐ **Respect:** Everyone is given the right to his or her own opinion, and all questions are encouraged and respected.
- ☐ **Confidentiality:** Anything that is said in the meeting is never repeated outside the meeting.
- ☐ **Life Change:** We will regularly assess our own life-change goals and encourage one another in our pursuit of Christlikeness.
- ☐ **Empty Chair:** The group stays open to reaching new people at every meeting.
- ☐ **Care and Support:** Permission is given to call upon each other at any time, especially in times of crisis. The group will provide care for every member.
- ☐ **Accountability:** We agree to let the members of the group hold us accountable to the commitments we make in whatever loving ways we decide upon.
- ☐ **Mission:** We will do everything in our power to start a new group.
- ☐ **Ministry:** The group will encourage one another to volunteer and serve in a ministry and to support missions by giving financially and/or personally serving.

notes

Session

1

A New Style of Leadership

1

Prepare for the Session

	READINGS	REFLECTIVE QUESTIONS
Monday	Luke 22:24	What church disputes have you gotten involved in recently? Do you feel you handled yourself in a way that honored Christ?
Tuesday	Luke 22:25	Are you trying to dominate someone right now to boost your own ego? In what way could you serve him or her instead?
Wednesday	Luke 22:26	In what ways are you trying to be "great" right now? Are you trying the world's way or Christ's way?
Thursday	Psalm 78:70-72	How has God used humbling situations in your past to shape you as a leader?
Friday	Psalm 119:125	How is God giving you discernment right now through what is happening to you?
Saturday	Proverbs 14:35	Are you valuing and seeking wisdom in all that you do?
Sunday	Matthew 24:42-46	If Christ returned today, would He say you have been faithful?

OUR GOALS FOR THIS SESSION ARE:

BIBLE STUDY

- To begin to see the difference between a dominating style of leadership and a servant style of leadership
- To understand the importance of working for God's glory rather than human praise
- To see Christ as our example for servant style leadership

LIFE CHANGE

- To do a caring act for someone anonymously
- To visit with a person with a low prestige job in your church or community
- To ask the youngest person in your household what we can do to be of service to them

Icebreaker

10-15 minutes

GATHERING THE PEOPLE:

Form horseshoe groups of 6-8.

"I Am the Greatest!" Depending on time, choose one or two questions, or answer all three. Go around the group on question 1 and let everyone share. Then go around again on question 2.

1. When you were in junior high school, what did you want to be "the greatest" at?

   - ☐ Sports
   - ☐ School
   - ☐ Singing
   - ☐ Playing in a band
   - ☐ Acting
   - ☐ Telling jokes
   - ☐ Impressing the opposite sex
   - ☐ Chess

2. Whom did you consider to be your biggest rival in doing what you mentioned in question 1? How did you act toward this rival?

3. When you were in junior high, what famous person do you remember looking up to as "the greatest" and why?

Bible Study

30-45 minutes

The Scripture for this week:

LEARNING FROM THE BIBLE

LUKE 22:24-27

24 Then a dispute also arose among them about who should be
considered the greatest. 25 But He said to them, "The kings of the
Gentiles dominate them, and those who have authority over them are
called 'Benefactors.' 26 But it must not be like that among you. On the
contrary, whoever is greatest among you must become like the
youngest, and whoever leads, like the one serving. 27 For who is
greater, the one at the table or the one serving? Isn't it the one at the
table? But I am among you as the One who serves.

...about today's session

A WORD FROM THE LEADER

Write your answers here.

1. What was the leadership problem Jesus was pointing out?

2. What actions typified the leadership style of Jesus' day?

3. What are three shortcomings of a leadership style typified by dominance?

____

____

____

Identifying with the Story

In horseshoe groups of 6–8, explore questions as time allows.

1. Over the course of your lifetime, who have you most often felt dominated by?
   - ☐ My parents
   - ☐ Male authority figures
   - ☐ Mother figures
   - ☐ The government
   - ☐ People with money
   - ☐ Nobody
   - ☐ Bullies – persons more violent than myself
   - ☐ Those in the popular crowd

2. What servant tasks were you most likely to have to do when you were young?
   - ☐ Wash the dishes
   - ☐ Cook meals
   - ☐ Clean the house
   - ☐ Do laundry
   - ☐ Do farm chores
   - ☐ Watch the younger children
   - ☐ Take out the trash

3. As an adult, when do you most feel like a servant?
   - ☐ Every time I pick up stuff in the house that someone else threw there
   - ☐ When the boss sends me for coffee
   - ☐ When I fix a meal that everyone else complains about
   - ☐ When I work such long hours that I have no time for fun
   - ☐ Whenever someone tells me to do something instead of asking me

today's session

What is God teaching you from this story?

1. Why was it important for Jesus to teach the disciples about leadership at this point in time?

2. What are three ways Christian leadership should differ from the style of leadership more typical of the world?

____

____

____

3. What does a dominant style of leadership breed? What examples are given concerning how this occurs? What other examples can you think of?

4. What does it mean that the Christian leader is to become "like the youngest"?

5. What are three ways Christ differed from human kings and governments?

____

____

____

Learning from the Story

In horseshoe groups of 6–8, choose an answer and explain why you chose what you did.

1. To whom are you trying to prove right now that you are "the greatest"?

- ☐ A parent
- ☐ A sibling
- ☐ My boss
- ☐ Myself
- ☐ An old boyfriend or girlfriend
- ☐ My spouse's parents
- ☐ Whoever will pay attention

LEARNING FROM THE STORY (cont'd)

2. What "first step" do you need to take to liberate yourself from the opinion of the person you chose in question 1?

3. Whom around you do you sometimes try to dominate? What would it mean for you to take on a servant style of leadership with this person?

life change lessons

How can you apply this session to your life?

Write your answers here.

1. What were three actions of Peter that showed he was slow to understand how to apply Christ's servant style of leadership?

____

____

____

2. What three Christian leaders are mentioned as having done a good job of living out Christ's servant style of leadership? Can you think of others?

____

____

____

Caring Time

15-20 minutes

CARING TIME

Remain in horseshoe groups of 6-8.

This is the time to develop and express your care for each other. Begin by having group members finish this sentence:

"What I hope to gain from this class is ..."

Pray for these hopes, as well as the concerns on the Prayer/ Praise Report. Include prayer for the empty chair.

If you would like to pray silently, say "Amen" when you have finished your prayer, so that the next person will know when to start.

Reference Notes

BIBLE STUDY NOTES

Use these notes to gain further understanding of the text as you study on your own.

LUKE 22:24-27 In a passage similar to Mark 10:37,41-45, Jesus pointed out that true greatness in God's kingdom is not a matter of status but service. John 13:1-7 records how Jesus enacted this principle at this very meal by adopting the position of a servant to wash the disciples' feet.

LUKE 22:24 ***among them.*** Matthew and Mark describe a similar dispute with James' and John's request for privilege at the heart of it (Matt. 20:20-28; Mark 10:35-45). ***who should be considered the greatest.*** While Jesus was seeking strength and support to face His own death, the disciples were thinking of themselves. Part of what needs to be understood here is that the disciples were probably still thinking that Jesus was going to be the Messiah as traditionally conceived. This would mean that He would establish a kingdom soon, and that His chief disciples would have great influence in that kingdom. "To the victors belong the spoils," and the disciples were wanting to know ahead of time who might get the greatest share.

LUKE 22:26 ***like the youngest.*** Prestige in this culture went with age and experience. The youngest people had little prestige or honor. Jesus' followers should not think that true greatness requires any more prestige than the youngest person received in that culture.

LUKE 22:27 ***For who is greater ...?*** The question Jesus raised is a rhetorical one concerning who is greater in the eyes of the world. That Jesus has come among them as one who serves indicates that what the world sees as greatness is not the same as what God sees as greatness.

notes

Session

2

A New Understanding of Humility

Prepare for the Session

	READINGS	REFLECTIVE QUESTIONS
Monday	Philippians 2:3	How would it affect what you do today if you could totally eliminate rivalry and conceit from your motivations?
Tuesday	Philippians 2:4	How are you doing balancing your own interests with the interests of others?
Wednesday	Philippians 2:5-8	When was the last time you thanked Christ for the sacrifice He made for you?
Thursday	Philippians 2:9-11	What are you doing to exalt the name of Christ?
Friday	Matthew 11:28-30	How does it give your spirit rest to not have to strive to be better than others?
Saturday	Matthew 22:34-40	How is being humble a part of loving God and others?
Sunday	James 4:10	How has Christ lifted you up when others have brought you low?

OUR GOALS FOR THIS SESSION ARE:

BIBLE STUDY

- To see the connection between servant leadership and being "a team player"
- To better understand what humility means in terms of balancing our interests with the interests of others
- To learn the importance of obedience to God as part of being a humble servant leader

LIFE CHANGE

- To talk to someone we don't know very well about what his or her needs are
- To examine a conflict that is occurring in our church right now so as to design a "win-win" proposal to address it
- To find one opportunity each day of this week to let someone know he or she is important to God

Icebreaker

10-15 minutes

GATHERING THE PEOPLE:

Form horseshoe groups of 6-8.

"Downwardly Mobile." Depending on time, choose one or two questions, or answer all three. Go around the group on question 1 and let everyone share. Then go around again on question 2.

1. When you were in high school, what group would you have considered it "lowering yourself" to be part of?

☐ The chess club
☐ The cheerleading squad
☐ The band
☐ The computer nerds
☐ The drop-outs
☐ Any group that didn't dress like "us"

2. Which of the following would you be least likely to "lower yourself" to do right now?

☐ Play the lottery
☐ Watch "reality" television
☐ Get a tattoo
☐ Watch Jerry Springer
☐ Wear clothes bought at Wal-Mart, K-Mart, or the like
☐ Buy a supermarket tabloid or "scandal sheet"

3. When have you thought that you were "lowering yourself" to do something, only to find out that you were glad you did?

Bible Study

30-45 minutes

The Scripture for this week:

LEARNING FROM THE BIBLE

PHILIPPIANS 2:1-11

1 If then there is any encouragement in Christ, if any consolation
of love, if any fellowship with the Spirit, if any affection and mercy,
2 fulfill my joy by thinking the same way, having the same love, shar-
ing the same feelings, focusing on one goal. 3 Do nothing out of rival-
ry or conceit, but in humility consider others as more important than
yourselves. 4 Everyone should look out not [only] for his own interests,
but also for the interests of others.

5 Make your own attitude that of Christ Jesus,
6 who, existing in the form of God, did not consider equality with
God as something to be used for His own advantage.
7 Instead He emptied Himself by assuming the form of a slave,
taking on the likeness of men.
And when He had come as a man in His external form,
8 He humbled Himself by becoming obedient
to the point of death—even to death on a cross.
9 For this reason God also highly exalted Him
and gave Him the name that is above every name,
10 so that at the name of Jesus every knee should bow—of those
who are in heaven and on earth and under the earth—
11 and every tongue should confess that Jesus Christ is Lord,
to the glory of God the Father.

...about today's session

A WORD FROM THE LEADER

Write your answers here.

1. What are three misconceptions about what *humility* means?

____

____

____

2. In what ways did Jesus behave that shows He did not agree with the misconceptions about humility referred to in question 1?

3. What two things did Jesus do to show true humility?

____

____

Identifying with the Story

In horseshoe groups of 6–8, explore questions as time allows.

1. In which of the following ways do you tend to get tied up in rivalries?

- ☐ Over sports – trash talking against my friends' teams.
- ☐ Over work – downplaying their accomplishments while highlighting my own.
- ☐ Over possessions – "keeping up with the Joneses" – and then some!
- ☐ Over fashion – "When I go out, people better be looking at *me*!"
- ☐ Over board or card games – "I'm not competitive! He/she is competitive!"
- ☐ Over knowledge of various subjects – always having to "prove 'em wrong."
- ☐ Over the attention of children – "I want them to love me the most!"

2. What are some of the "interests" you have that you tend to look out for? How would you describe your own interests in relation to the following areas?

Your ambitions ______________________________.

Your own security ___________________________.

Your reputation _____________________________.

Your possessions ____________________________.

3. When it comes to looking out for the interests of others, what is the biggest challenge you have?

☐ Understanding what those interests are.
☐ Balancing my interests with theirs.
☐ It goes against my corporate training: to focus on achieving our objectives.
☐ It goes against my philosophy of "survival of the fittest."
☐ Who has the time to figure it all out?
☐ I don't feel it is a challenge.

today's session

What is God teaching you from this story?

1. Why is it significant that when Paul wrote this passage, he was imprisoned in Rome?

2. What are three things this passage suggests we do to model ourselves after Christ and become servant leaders?

____

____

____

3. What goal does Paul say he was striving for later in Philippians?

TODAY'S SESSION (cont'd)

4. What three passages are referred to that affirm that we are all valuable before God?

   ____

   ____

   ____

5. Why is it significant that even Jesus was obedient to God the Father?

Learning from the Story

In horseshoe groups of 6–8, choose an answer and explain why you chose what you did.

1. Using the scale below each item, how would you grade the church you are part of on each of these instructions of Paul?

   "thinking the same way" (having a similar theological perspective)

   1 · · · 2 · · · 3 · · · 4 · · · 5 · · · 6 · · · 7 · · · 8 · · · 9 · · · 10
   Not at all true — Very much true

   "having the same love" (all are included, little favoritism)

   1 · · · 2 · · · 3 · · · 4 · · · 5 · · · 6 · · · 7 · · · 8 · · · 9 · · · 10
   Not at all true — Very much true

   "sharing the same feelings" (get excited and passionate about the same ministries)

   1 · · · 2 · · · 3 · · · 4 · · · 5 · · · 6 · · · 7 · · · 8 · · · 9 · · · 10
   Not at all true — Very much true

   "focusing on one goal" (heading in the same direction, not "butting heads")

   1 · · · 2 · · · 3 · · · 4 · · · 5 · · · 6 · · · 7 · · · 8 · · · 9 · · · 10
   Not at all true — Very much true

2. When was the last time you can remember struggling to decide between your own interests and the interests of others? What did you end up doing, and how did you decide?

3. Christ gave up His place in heaven and ultimately His earthly life in order to be obedient. Which of the following do you have the hardest time giving up in order to be obedient to God's direction?

- ☐ Status
- ☐ Physical safety
- ☐ Emotional safety
- ☐ Material possession
- ☐ Physical comfort
- ☐ Friendship

2

life change lessons

How can you apply this session to your life?

Write your answers here.

1. What are two ways to "lose our balance" in our efforts to show biblical humility?

____

____

2. What are three biblical examples of how Jesus sought to get others to share with Him what their needs were?

____

____

____

Caring Time

15-20 minutes

CARING TIME

Remain in horseshoe groups of 6-8.

This is the time to develop and express your care for each other. Begin by having group members respond to this question:

"What 'encouragement in Christ' are you especially needing right now?"

Pray for these needs, as well as the concerns on the Prayer/ Praise Report. Include prayer for the empty chair.

If you would like to pray silently, say "Amen" when you have finished your prayer, so that the next person will know when to start.

Reference Notes

BIBLE STUDY NOTES

Use these notes to gain further understanding of the text as you study on your own.

PHILIPPIANS 2:1

By means of four clauses, Paul urged the Philippians to say "Yes" to his request that they live together in harmony. They had a strong incentive to be united to one another because of their experience of the encouragement, love, fellowship, mercy, and compassion of God the Father, Son, and Holy Spirit.

if. In Greek, this construction assumes a positive response, e.g., "If you have an encouragement, as of course you do ..."

PHILIPPIANS 2:2

thinking the same way. Paul was not just urging everyone to hold identical ideas and opinions. The word for *think* is far more comprehensive and involves not only one's mind, but one's feelings, attitudes, and will. Paul was calling for a far deeper form of unity than simple doctrinal conformity.

sharing the same feelings. In Greek, this is a single word that Paul probably made up since it is found nowhere else.

PHILIPPIANS 2:3

rivalry. This is the second time Paul has used this word (see note on 1:17 in session 2). It means working to advance oneself without thought for others.

conceit. This is the only occurrence of this word in the New Testament. Translated literally, it means "vain glory" *(kenodoxia)* which is asserting oneself over God who alone is worthy of true glory *(doxa)*. This is the sort of person who will arrogantly assert that he or she is right even through what that person holds is false. This is a person whose concern is for personal prestige.

PHILIPPIANS 2:3 (cont'd)

humility. This was not a virtue the Greek valued in the first century. They considered this to be the attitude of a slave, i.e., servility. In the Old Testament, however, this was understood to be the proper attitude to hold before God. Christians are to accord others the same dignity and respect that Christ has given to all people. Humility involves seeing others not on the basis of how clever, attractive, or pious they are, but through the eyes of Christ (who died for them).

PHILIPPIANS 2:4

for his own interests. Preoccupation with personal interests, along with selfish ambition and vain conceit, make unity impossible. Individualism or partisanship work against community. Note that Paul says "look not only to your own interests." Personal interests are important (although not to the exclusion of everything else).

2

PHILIPPIANS 2:5

This is a transitional verse in which Paul states that the model for the sort of self-sacrificing humility he has been urging is found in Jesus.

PHILIPPIANS 2:6-11

There is little agreement between scholars as to how this hymn breaks into verses or how it is to be phrased. However, one thing is clear. The hymn has two equal parts. Part one (vv. 6-8) focuses on the self-humiliation of Jesus. Part two (vv. 9-11) focuses on God's exaltation of Jesus. In part one, Jesus is the subject of the two main verbs, while in part two, God is the subject of the two main verbs.

PHILIPPIANS 2:6

the form of God. The Greek word here is *morphe* (used twice by Paul in this hymn). He says that Jesus was in His nature (form) God, but that He then took upon Himself the form or nature of a servant (v. 7). This is a key word in understanding the nature of Christ. Jesus possessed the essential nature of God. Why didn't Paul say this more directly? In the same way that a Jew could not bring himself to pronounce the name of God, a strict monotheist like Paul could not quite bring himself to say bluntly: "Jesus is God," though he winds up saying this very thing.
to be used for His advantage. This translates a rare word, used only at this point in the New Testament. The Holman translation points out that while Jesus was God, he did not look upon that as something to exempt him from the possibility of human suffering.

PHILIPPIANS 2:7

emptied himself. Literally, "to pour out until the container is empty." This could be interpreted to mean that Christ stripped Himself of all of the "rights and privileges" that would normally come with His status, so that He might face life with the same disadvantages as the rest of us human beings.
assuming the form of a slave. Jesus gave up Godhood and took on slavehood. From being the ultimate master, He became the lowest slave. He left ruling for serving. *Morphe* is used here again, indicating that Jesus adopted the essential nature of a slave.
taking on the likeness of men. The point is not that Jesus just seemed to be human. He assumed the identity of a person and was similar in all ways to other human beings.

REFERENCE NOTES PHILIPPIANS 2:7 (cont'd)

as a man in His external form. The word translated "external form" is *schema*, and denotes that which is outward and changeable (over against *morphe*, which denotes that which is essential and eternal.) In other words, Jesus was a true man, but only temporarily.

PHILIPPIANS 2:8

He humbled Himself. This is the central point that Paul wanted to make. This is why he offered this illustration. Jesus is the ultimate model of one who lived a life of self-sacrifice, self-renunciation, and self-surrender. Jesus existed at the pinnacle and yet descended to the very base. There has never been a more radical humbling. Furthermore, this was not something forced upon Jesus. Christ voluntarily chose to humble Himself.

obedient to the point of death. This clause defines the extent of this humbling. Jesus humbled himself to the furthest point one could go. He submitted to death itself for the sake of both God and humanity. There was no more dramatic way to demonstrate humility.

death on a cross. This was no ordinary death. For one thing, it came about in an unusually cruel way. Crucifixion was a harsh, demeaning, and utterly painful way to die. For another thing, according to the Old Testament, those who died by hanging on a tree were considered to have been cursed by God. For a Jew there was no more humiliating way to die. Jesus, who was equal to God, died like a condemned criminal. His descent from glory had brought him as low as one could go.

PHILIPPIANS 2:9

Jesus' self-humiliation is followed by His God-induced exaltation. Jesus descended to the depths and was raised again to the heights.

Name. In the ancient world, a name was more than just a way of distinguishing one individual from another. It revealed the inner nature or character of a person. The name given the resurrected Jesus is the supreme name – the name above all names – because this is who Jesus is in His innermost being.

PHILIPPIANS 2:10

Jesus. It is significant that the one before whom all will bow is Jesus, the man from Nazareth. The cosmic Lord is none other than the person who walked the roads of Palestine and talked to the people of Israel. He had a hometown, a family, a trade, and disciples. The one before whom Christians will stand at the last judgment is not an anonymous life force, but the man of Galilee who has a familiar face.

PHILIPPIANS 2:11

Jesus Christ is Lord. Here is the climax of this hymn. This is the earliest and most basic confession of faith on the part of the church (see Acts 2:36; Rom. 10:9; 1 Cor. 12:3).

notes

notes

Session

3 The Power in Servanthood

Prepare for the Session

	READINGS	REFLECTIVE QUESTIONS
Monday	Matthew 21:1-3	How willing are you to give to the Lord what He has need of?
Tuesday	Matthew 21:6-9	Are you publicly praising the name of Jesus? In what ways?
Wednesday	Matthew 21:10-11	In what way has Jesus "shaken you up"?
Thursday	Acts 17:5-8	In what way is the church you are part of "turning the world upside down"? If they aren't, why aren't they?
Friday	Luke 22:28-30	Do you have the courage to stand by Christ when His name is being slandered?
Saturday	Romans 10:9-11	Are you proclaiming Christ as Lord with your mouth as well as your behavior?
Sunday	Revelation 19:11-16	How would it affect how you behaved today if you knew tomorrow would be the day Jesus Christ would come and reign throughout creation?

OUR GOALS FOR THIS SESSION ARE:

BIBLE STUDY

- To explore what role power plays in leadership, particularly for the servant leader that Christ calls us to be
- To see how Christ was a different kind of king or leader than the people were expecting
- To appreciate the power Christ had and how He used it

LIFE CHANGE

- To ask two persons who know us well for their honest feedback on how we use power
- To take our primary leadership role and write our own mission statement for that role
- To take one action this week to use our power to influence the values of others to be more Christ-like

Icebreaker

10-15 minutes

GATHERING THE PEOPLE:

Form horseshoe groups of 6-8.

"I Love a Parade!" Depending on time, choose one or two questions, or answer all three. Go around the group on question 1 and let everyone share. Then go around again on question 2.

1. When you were a child, what parade do you most remember watching? What was your favorite part?

2. If you could magically be granted whatever ability you needed, what role would you most like to take in a parade?

   ☐ The leader of the marching band
   ☐ One of those who get to bang on the drums
   ☐ The beauty queen waving from the float
   ☐ The clown making the children laugh and passing out candy
   ☐ The guy who walks around on stilts
   ☐ The parade marshal or dignitary who gets to ride in the limo
   ☐ Part of a precision marching team
   ☐ A designer of the floats
   ☐ One who gets to ride a horse

3. If you could design a parade float to celebrate the best thing in your life right now, what would it be like? What would be your float's "theme"?

Bible Study

30-45 minutes

The Scripture for this week:

LEARNING FROM THE BIBLE

MATTHEW 21:1-11

[1]When they approached Jerusalem and came to Bethphage at the
Mount of Olives, Jesus then sent two disciples, [2]telling them, "Go into
the village ahead of you. At once you will find a donkey tied there,
and a colt with her. Untie them and bring them to Me. [3]If anyone
says anything to you, you should say that the Lord needs them, and
immediately he will send them."

[4]This took place so that what was spoken through the prophet
might be fulfilled:

[5]Tell Daughter Zion,
"See, your King is coming to you,
gentle, and mounted on a donkey,
even on a colt, the foal of a beast of burden."

[6]The disciples went and did just as Jesus directed them. [7]They
brought the donkey and the colt, laid their robes on them, and He sat
on them. [8]A very large crowd spread their robes on the road; others
were cutting branches from the trees and spreading them on the road.
[9]Then the crowds who went before Him and those who followed kept
shouting:

Hosanna to the Son of David!
Blessed is He who comes in the name of the Lord!
Hosanna in the highest heaven!

[10]When He entered Jerusalem, the whole city was shaken, saying,
"Who is this?" [11]And the crowds kept saying, "This is the prophet
Jesus from Nazareth in Galilee!"

...about today's session

A WORD FROM THE LEADER

Write your answers here.

1. What was the significance of spreading clothing and tree branches on the road before Jesus' path?

2. What was the significance of the fact that Jesus rode into Jerusalem on a donkey and not a war horse?

3. What were three kinds of power that Jesus manifested as He came into Jerusalem on Palm Sunday?

   ____

   ____

   ____

Identifying with the Story

In horseshoe groups of 6–8, explore questions as time allows.

1. When you make your entrance at a party, what are you most likely to do?
   - ☐ Come fashionably late and grab everyone's attention
   - ☐ Come early and help with the work
   - ☐ Slip in when no one is looking
   - ☐ Come in with my spouse and have him/her run interference for me
   - ☐ Scout out who is there before making my move

2. When have you felt most honored by a group you were part of (a family gathering, a church group, business associates, a sports team, etc.)? What was the occasion and how did you feel about it?

3. When you are honored or praised, which of the following are you most likely to do?

- ☐ Put myself down as unworthy
- ☐ Deflect the attention to someone else as soon as possible
- ☐ Try to figure out what the brown-nosers are trying to get from me
- ☐ Enjoy it while I can
- ☐ Soak it up and look for more

today's session

What is God teaching you from this story?

1. What kind of prophecy were the people of Jerusalem hoping Jesus had come to fulfill?

2. What did Roman conquerors build to commemorate their victories? What is a good example of this?

3. What examples of changed lives are listed as evidence of Christ's power?

____

____

____

____

4. What are five areas of life where Christ has changed societal values down through time?

____

____

____

____

____

TODAY'S SESSION (cont'd)

5. Why was Christ's power greater than that of a military ruler?

Learning from the Story

In horseshoe groups of 6–8, choose an answer and explain why you chose what you did.

1. If you knew that Christ was going to come into your city tomorrow, what would be the number one thing you would want to do to prepare the way for Him?

2. When Christ entered Jerusalem and someone asked who He was, the crowd answered by giving His name, and saying He was a prophet. What would you say? Which of the following says the most to you about who Jesus was?

   - ☐ Son of God
   - ☐ Prophet
   - ☐ Savior of the world
   - ☐ Friend of sinners
   - ☐ Teacher of Righteousness
   - ☐ Servant King

3. What can you do to make sure the way you present yourself as a leader reflects the Christ who rode into Jerusalem on a humble servant animal?

life change lessons

How can you apply this session to your life?

Write your answers here.

1. Why would most people think of the term "powerful servant" as an oxymoron? What did Christ do to show this is a viable term?

2. What are three things Christians should learn about leadership from Christ's entrance on Palm Sunday?

Caring Time

15-20 minutes

CARING TIME

Remain in horseshoe groups of 6-8.

This is the time to develop and express your care for each other. Begin by having group members respond to this question:

"Were Christ to enter your town today, what words of praise would you want to shout out to Him?"

Include these words of praise in your prayer, and then pray about the concerns on the Prayer/ Praise Report. Include prayer for the empty chair.

If you would like to pray silently, say "Amen" when you have finished your prayer, so that the next person will know when to start.

3

Reference Notes

BIBLE STUDY NOTES

Use these notes to gain further understanding of the text as you study on your own.

MATTHEW 21:1

Jerusalem. This was the central city in Palestine and the spiritual heart of Israel. At the feasts (especially Passover), the population of Jerusalem would be swelled by Jews who made pilgrimage from all over the known world.
Bethphage. This was a village near Bethany, two miles east of Jerusalem.
Mount of Olives. According to Zechariah 14:4-5, this was the place where God would commence the final judgment of Israel's enemies.
Jesus then sent. Clearly Jesus was consciously preparing His entry. His manner of arrival was meant to be a sign of who He is.

MATTHEW 21:2

donkey ... colt. Matthew's reference to two animals (a donkey and a colt) on which Jesus would ride could possibly be based on a misunderstanding of the passage from Zechariah 9:9. There the reference is "on a donkey, on a colt the foal of a donkey." The original reference wasn't to two animals, but rather was a case of poetic parallelism. The second phrase merely made the second more specific. Mark (Mark 11:4-7) and Luke (Luke 19:30-36) refer to just one animal. Jesus would not simply walk into Jerusalem like the other pilgrims. He would come riding as the messianic King, in accordance with the prophecy of Zechariah. Riding a donkey emphasized the peaceful, gentle nature of the Messiah.

REFERENCE NOTES (cont'd)

MATTHEW 21:3

if anyone says anything to you. The words the disciples were to say would identify them to the owner as those Jesus had sent.

the Lord. Thus far in Matthew's Gospel, Jesus had not referred to himself by this title. While it can simply be a formal term for a master, the context of this occasion indicates he was implying divine authority as well.

MATTHEW 21:8

spread their robes. This was a gesture of respect, given to kings (2 Kings 9:12-13), prophets and other holy men.

cutting branches from the trees. John is the only one of the Gospels that specifically refers to palm branches (John 12:13.)

MATTHEW 21:9

Hosanna. Literally, "Save now!" This was commonly used as an expression of praise to God or as a greeting.

Son of David. King David was considered to be the model king of Israel. It was through his line that God had promised to build an everlasting kingdom.

Blessed is He. While the Psalm from which this cry is taken (Psa. 118:26) originally served as a tribute to the king of Israel, it was applied to any pilgrim who traveled to Jerusalem for the feasts. It was later understood by the rabbis to be a messianic psalm, referring to the final redemption that would be ushered in by the Messiah.

notes

notes

Session

4 The Suffering in Servanthood

Prepare for the Session

	READINGS	REFLECTIVE QUESTIONS
Monday	Isaiah 53:2	How much do you emphasize physical appearance over character and spiritual depth?
Tuesday	Isaiah 53:3	How do you deal with rejection? How does it affect you that Christ had to experience the same thing?
Wednesday	Isaiah 53:4-5	How does it make you feel that Christ suffered and died for you? What can you do to show your gratitude?
Thursday	Isaiah 53:6	When have you gone your own way to your own hurt? What have you learned from such times of wandering?
Friday	Isaiah 53:7	When have you opened your mouth when you should have kept silent, and when have you kept silent when you should have said something?
Saturday	Isaiah 53:10	Have you ever felt like God wanted you to suffer? Did you see much purpose in your suffering at the time?
Sunday	Isaiah 53:12	When have you been "counted among the rebels"? Are the things you have rebelled against what Christ would also have rebelled against?

OUR GOALS FOR THIS SESSION ARE:

BIBLE STUDY

- To explore how Christ was rejected and to better understand what that means when we are rejected
- To understand how Christ's suffering makes it so He can empathize with our suffering
- To consider the need for us to testify to the meaning of Christ's suffering

LIFE CHANGE

- To visit with someone at our church who has recently lost a loved one and to empathize with them
- To take action on behalf of someone who has experienced injustice
- To share with a non-believer the meaning of Christ's suffering

Icebreaker

10-15 minutes

GATHERING THE PEOPLE:

Form horseshoe groups of 6-8.

A Matter of Appearance. Depending on time, choose one or two questions, or answer all three. Go around the group on question 1 and let everyone share. Then go around again on question 2.

1. When you were in junior high, what part of your appearance did you feel might make people reject you?

- ☐ My acne
- ☐ My crooked teeth
- ☐ My weight
- ☐ My lack of height
- ☐ My small breast size
- ☐ My appearance in general
- ☐ My hair – it was always acting up
- ☐ My puny muscles – the proverbial 98-pound weakling

2. When you were in junior high, what part of your appearance did you take pride in and want everyone to notice?

- ☐ My eyes
- ☐ My figure/build
- ☐ My hair
- ☐ My smile
- ☐ My complexion
- ☐ My face

3. When in your life do you remember having had an experience or having met a person where you learned that appearance isn't everything?

Bible Study

30-45 minutes

The Scripture for this week:

LEARNING FROM THE BIBLE

ISAIAH 53:1-12

4

1 Who has believed what we have heard?
And who has the arm of the LORD been revealed to?
2 He grew up before Him like a young plant.
And like a root out of dry ground.
He had no form or splendor that we should look at Him,
no appearance that we should desire Him.
3 He was despised and rejected by men,
a man of sufferings who knew what sickness was.
He was like one people turned away from;
He was despised, and we didn't value Him.
4 Yet He Himself bore our sicknesses,
And He carried our pains;
but we in turn regarded Him stricken,
struck down by God, and afflicted.
5 But He was pierced because of our transgressions,
crushed because of our iniquities;
punishment for our peace was on Him,
and we are healed by His wounds.
6 We all went astray like sheep;
we all have turned to our own way;
and the LORD has punished Him
for the iniquity of us all.
7 He was oppressed and afflicted,
Yet He did not open His mouth.
Like a lamb led to the slaughter
And like a sheep silent before her shearers,
He did not open His mouth.

BIBLE STUDY (cont'd)

8 *He was taken away because of oppression and judgment;*
and who considered His fate?
For He was cut off from the land of the living;
He was struck because of My people's rebellion.
9 *They made His grave with the wicked,*
and with a rich man at His death,
although He had done no violence
and had not spoken deceitfully.
10 *Yet the LORD was pleased to crush Him,*
and He made Him sick.
When You make Him a restitution offering,
He will see [His] seed, He will prolong His days,
and the will of the LORD will succeed by His hand.
11 *He will see [it] out of His anguish,*
and He will be satisfied with His knowledge.
My righteous servant will justify many,
and He will carry their iniquities.
12 *Therefore I will give Him the many as a portion,*
and He will receive the mighty as spoil,
because He submitted Himself to death,
and was counted among the rebels;
Yet He bore the sin of many
and interceded for the rebels.

...about today's session

A WORD FROM THE LEADER

Write your answers here.

1. Who does the servant appear to be in passages such as Isaiah 41 and 44?

2. Why cannot the servant referred to in Isaiah 49 be the nation of Israel?

3. What does Isaiah 53 describe as the central act of the servant?

Identifying with the Story

In horseshoe groups of 6–8, explore questions as time allows.

1. When have you most felt "despised and rejected"?
   - ☐ When I was a child and didn't get much attention from my parents
   - ☐ When I was in high school and had few dates
   - ☐ When I was applying for jobs and kept getting turned down
   - ☐ When I went through divorce
   - ☐ When I had to make some unpopular decisions
   - ☐ When my children became teenagers
   - ☐ All the time
   - ☐ I have never felt that way

2. When was there a period in your life when you "went astray"? Was it a moral wandering, a spiritual wandering, or a professional detour? What got you back on track?

3. When you go through a difficult time, are you more likely to keep silent and try to manage it yourself, or talk about it to everyone who will listen? Rate yourself on the following scale:

   1 · · · 2 · · · 3 · · · 4 · · · 5 · · · 6 · · · 7 · · · 8 · · · 9 · · · 10

   A quiet little lamb — Roaring like a tiger!

4

today's session

What is God teaching you from this story?

1. What New Testament passage is quoted to show that Jesus was rejected in the manner that was prophesied in Isaiah 53?

2. Why should Christians expect to be rejected sometimes?

TODAY'S SESSION (cont'd)

3. What are four experiences Jesus had that help us know that He went through many of the difficult things we must go through?

____

____

____

____

4. What are three things that happened in Jesus' trial before Pilate that make it evident that He was the victim of injustice?

____

____

____

5. What should be our ultimate goal as Christian servant leaders?

Learning from the Story

In horseshoe groups of 6–8, choose an answer and explain why you chose what you did.

1. When you think about the times you have "gone astray," what does this passage say to you that might keep such times from recurring?

2. Looking at this passage, what is the next thing you need to do to really find healing from your spiritual wounds?
   - ☐ "Believe what I have heard" about Christ's act of redemption
   - ☐ Stop focusing on my own experiences of rejection, and focus more on Christ's
   - ☐ Stop punishing myself for that for which Christ has already suffered
   - ☐ Stop doing things that make Christ suffer even more
   - ☐ other: ______________________________

3. Finish this sentence: "When I think about what Christ did in suffering for me, it makes me want to ..."

life change lessons

How can you apply this session to your life?

Write your answers here.

1. What are three destructive choices a person can make in relation to dealing with the suffering they go through?

   ____

   ____

   ____

2. What is the more positive choice a Christian can make to deal with his or her suffering?

4

Caring Time

15-20 minutes

CARING TIME

Remain in horseshoe groups of 6-8.

This is the time to develop and express your caring for each other. Begin by having group members respond to this question:

"In what way are you experiencing suffering right now?"

Include these needs and concerns in your prayer, and then pray about the concerns on the Prayer/ Praise Report. Include prayer for the empty chair.

If you would like to pray silently, say "Amen" when you have finished your prayer, so that the next person will know when to start.

BIBLE STUDY NOTES

Reference Notes

Use these notes to gain further understanding of the text as you study on your own.

ISAIAH 53:2 ***a young plant ... like a root out of dry ground.*** This connotes life coming from where life would not be expected to come—dry, arid ground. Christ did not come from an environment a person of the time might have expected for the Messiah. He was not born of a royal or priestly family. He did not have formal training in the Torah. Adding to this, the religious authorities of the day rejected Him. Yet out of this "dry ground" God brought the one of whom John said, "In Him was life, and that life was the light of men" (John 1:4).

ISAIAH 53:4 ***He Himself bore our sicknesses.*** The nation of Israel will realize that the servant took upon Himself the consequences of their sin, an illness of the soul.

ISAIAH 53:5 ***crushed because of our iniquities.*** Like grapes were crushed to make wine, the servant was crushed. The servant suffered in our place to reconcile us with God. He healed physical illnesses during His earthly ministry, and through His suffering He healed spiritual illness as well.

ISAIAH 53:6 ***We all went astray like sheep.*** In this culture, this would have been a very familiar image. Sheep were prone to wandering off. Jesus later told a parable of how a good shepherd would leave 99 sheep in the open country to go search for one who had wandered off and become lost (Luke15:1-7). The mentioning of "sheep" also sets up the references to the servant's role as sacrificial lamb.

punished Him for the iniquity of us all. The idea that the sin or guilt or one life can be placed on another was well established in the Israelite faith, as the sins of the people were placed ceremoniously on a sacrificial lamb before it was slaughtered. This is what God did, using His own spotless Son, instead of a spotless lamb. Believers are to admit their guilt and acknowledge that the Lord suffered punishment and death in their place.

ISAIAH 53:7 ***Like a lamb led to the slaughter.*** Another allusion to Christ's role as sacrificial lamb.

ISAIAH 53:9 ***a rich man.*** The wealthy Joseph of Arimathea provided the tomb for Jesus' burial (Matt. 27:57-60).

ISAIAH 53:10 ***When you make Him a restitution offering.*** This referred to the doctrine of the atonement, or substitute sacrifice as payment for sin. Jesus' death satisfied the penalty for sin, and allowed all who accept His sacrifice in faith to be reconciled to God (2 Cor. 5:21).

ISAIAH 53:12 ***receive the mighty as spoil.*** This verse depicts a victorious army general sharing the enemy's goods with his soldiers. Believers will share in the benefits of Christ's rewards.

notes

4

notes

Session

5

The Self-Assurance in Servanthood

Prepare for the Session

	READINGS	REFLECTIVE QUESTIONS
Monday	John 13:3	How clear is your understanding of where you are going in life? What could give you a clearer sense of direction?
Tuesday	John 13:6-8	In what ways are you pushing Jesus away and keeping Him from touching you?
Wednesday	John 13:10-11	What part of your life needs to be "cleaned up"? What first step do you need to take for this to happen?
Thursday	John 13:12-15	What "servant tasks" are you doing to show love to the people around you?
Friday	2 Timothy 2:23	How easily are you hooked into destructive arguments? How does this affect your witness?
Saturday	2 Timothy 2:24-26	How does self-assurance help you to think in terms of serving an opponent instead of having to "win" over him or her?
Sunday	Philippians 4:13	How confident are you of your ability to do what God has called you to do? What would help you have greater confidence?

OUR GOALS FOR THIS SESSION ARE:

BIBLE STUDY

- To gain a greater understanding of what was at the core of Jesus Christ's self-assurance
- To appreciate the importance of self-assurance to acting as a servant leader
- To better understand what Jesus did when He washed His disciples' feet and to think of modern equivalents so that we might walk in His steps

LIFE CHANGE

- To volunteer one evening this week to wash the feet of all who live in our household
- To investigate the gifts that God has given us
- To write our life mission statement

Icebreaker

10-15 minutes

GATHERING THE PEOPLE:

Form horseshoe groups of 6-8.

Our Roots. Depending on time, choose one or two questions, or answer all three. Go around the group on question 1 and let everyone share. Then go around again on question 2.

1. Which of the following nationalities are included in your ancestry?

☐ English, Irish, or Scottish
☐ European – French, German, or Swiss
☐ European – Italian or Greek
☐ Hispanic or Latin American
☐ Asian – Japanese, Chinese, or Korean
☐ Asian – Indian or Pakistani
☐ Asian – Cambodian, Thai, or Vietnamese
☐ other: ____________________
☐ African
☐ Scandinavian
☐ Native American
☐ Russian or Slavic
☐ An island culture

2. What personality traits do you have that family members tell you make you like a parent or grandparent?

3. How do you feel your roots affect who you are?

- ☐ Not at all
- ☐ Perhaps in some indiscernible way
- ☐ It affects my temperament
- ☐ It affects my self-identity
- ☐ It affects the way people treat me
- ☐ It affects every aspect of who I am

Bible Study

30-45 minutes

The Scripture for this week:

LEARNING FROM THE BIBLE

JOHN 13:2-17

5

*[2]Now by the time of supper, the Devil had already put it into the
heart of Judas, Simon Iscariot's son, to betray Him. [3]Jesus knew that
the Father had given everything into His hands, that He had come
from God, and that He was going back to God. [4]So He got up from
supper, laid aside His robe, took a towel, and tied it around Himself.
[5]Next, He poured water into a basin and began to wash His disciples'
feet and to dry them with the towel tied around Him.*

[6]He came to Simon Peter, who asked Him, "Lord, are You going to wash my feet?"

[7]Jesus answered him, "What I'm doing you don't understand now, but afterward you will know."

[8]"You will never wash my feet—ever!" Peter said.

Jesus replied, "If I don't wash you, you have no part with Me."

[9]Simon Peter said to Him, "Lord, not only my feet, but also my hands and my head."

*[10]"One who has bathed," Jesus told him, "doesn't need to wash
anything except his feet, but he is completely clean. You are clean,
but not all of you." [11]For He knew who would betray Him. This is
why He said, "You are not all clean."*

*[12]When Jesus had washed their feet and put on His robe, He
reclined again and said to them, "Do you know what I have done
for you? [13]You call Me Teacher and Lord. This is well said, for I am.*

BIBLE STUDY (cont'd)

14So if I, your Lord and Teacher, have washed your feet, you also ought to wash one another's feet. 15For I have given you an example that you also should do just as I have done for you.

16"I assure you: A slave is not greater than his master, and a messenger is not greater than the one who sent him. 17If you know these things, you are blessed if you do them.

...about today's session

A WORD FROM THE LEADER

Write your answers here.

1. What were three things Christ knew about Himself, and which helped Him have self-assurance?

____

____

____

2. Why hadn't one of the disciples taken on the task of washing the feet of the others?

3. What should our attitude be about ourselves when we are serving others?

Identifying with the Story

In horseshoe groups of 6–8, explore questions as time allows.

1. When you were a teenager, which of the following "servant tasks" do you remember having to do for other members of the family? Check the tasks you had to do. Also put an exclamation mark next to the one you liked doing the most, and an X next to the one you wished you didn't have to do:

____ Changing diapers for a baby
____ Giving a toddler a bath
____ Feeding a baby or toddler
____ Baby-sitting younger brothers and sisters

____ Taking care of a family member when they were sick
____ Cutting or fixing the hair of a sibling
____ Giving back rubs or foot massages to other members of the family
____ Taking care of an older family member, like a grandparent or great-grandparent
____ other: ______________________________

2. When, if ever, have you had the experience of wanting to take care of someone who refused to let you help? How did you feel at the time? Did they ever change their mind?

3. Of the three things that Jesus knew about Himself, which do you struggle with the most?
   - ☐ "that the Father had given everything into His hands" – I really don't have a clear view of how God has gifted me or of what He wants me to do with those gifts.
   - ☐ "that He had come from God" – I feel disconnected from my "roots," the traditions and family that helped form me.
   - ☐ "that he was going back to God" – I have no idea where I am going in life!

today's session

What is God teaching you from this story?

1. What is the most important key to knowing who we are?

2. What two biblical examples are given of how God can help a person find greater self-assurance?

____

____

TODAY'S SESSION (cont'd)

3. What does it mean that God had "put everything into [Jesus'] hands"?

4. True self-assurance comes from knowing what two truths?

 ____

 ____

5. How should we as Christians be using our gifts?

Learning from the Story

In horseshoe groups of 6–8, choose an answer and explain why you chose what you did.

1. Had Jesus come up to you to wash your feet, which of the following would most likely have been your reaction?
   - ☐ The same as Peter's – "You will never wash my feet—ever!"
   - ☐ I would have just died of embarrassment.
   - ☐ I would have offered to wash people's feet in His stead.
   - ☐ I would have just started crying, then and there.
   - ☐ I would have been overwhelmed with a feeling of love and humility.

2. What do Jesus' words, "If I don't wash you, you have no part with Me" say to you?
   - ☐ I have to be able to receive loving acts as well as giving them.
   - ☐ I have to be spiritually cleansed by Jesus.
   - ☐ Baptism is an essential expression of faith.
   - ☐ Peter needed to cooperate so Jesus could teach His lesson.
   - ☐ other: ______________________________

3. What do you need to learn from this story that helps you become a better servant leader?
   - ☐ That Jesus has entrusted me with spiritual gifts and a mission
   - ☐ That I have to stop thinking it's all about me

- ☐ That there is no shame in doing humble tasks
- ☐ That sometimes you have to receive from others
- ☐ That it all starts with receiving the spiritual cleansing Christ gives
- ☐ That true self-assurance means not having to prove myself
- ☐ other: ______________________________

life change lessons

How can you apply this session to your life?

Write your answers here.

1. Why are attitude changes sometimes hard to make? What personal example can you give of this?

2. What are two things you can do to investigate the gifts God has given you?

   ____

   ____

5

Caring Time

15-20 minutes

CARING TIME

Remain in horseshoe groups of 6-8.

This is the time to develop and express your caring for each other. In the spirit of this week's lesson you may want to start with a modern equivalent of foot washing – the backrub! Pair up and have everyone give their partner a back-rub for a minute or two. Then have group members respond to this question:

"How can this group serve you in prayer this week?"

Include these needs and concerns in your prayer, and then pray about the concerns on the Prayer/ Praise Report. Include prayer for the empty chair.

If you would like to pray silently, say "Amen" when you have finished your prayer, so that the next person will know when to start.

BIBLE STUDY NOTES

Reference Notes

Use these notes to gain further understanding of the text as you study on your own.

JOHN 13:3 Jesus' self-knowledge was at the heart of His willingness to serve. This verse says that He knew who He was in terms of where He had come from (God), where He was going (back to God), and what His role was while He was here.

JOHN 13:4-5 Normally people's dusty, sandaled feet were washed by the lowest-ranking servant of the household before a meal was served. Jesus' action was deliberate. Removing His outer clothing was a sign He was going to do some work. It also would have identified Him with a servant who generally worked in minimal garb. The other Gospels mention that at the Last Supper the Twelve discussed who was the greatest (Luke 22:24). In that context, Jesus identified the greatest as the one who was the servant (Luke 22:25-26).

JOHN 13:6 ***Lord, are You going to wash my feet?*** Peter recognizing the impropriety of a master washing the servants' feet, protests. The Greek sentence actually reads more like "You? Wash my feet?" Peter is appalled at this breach of normal procedure.

JOHN 13:7 ***afterward you will know.*** This may simply be referring to verse 17, but more likely it refers to the full understanding of Jesus' servanthood that would be made clear after His resurrection.

JOHN 13:8 ***If I don't wash you, you have no part with Me.*** This adds another level of meaning to Jesus' act, in addition to that of an object lesson in humility. Jesus' foot washing was also a symbol of the spiritual cleansing He would accomplish for His followers through the Cross.

JOHN 13:10 ***One who has bathed.*** Jesus used the picture of a person who, after washing completely, travels somewhere. Upon arrival, only his feet need to be washed to be clean again.

You are clean, but not all of you. Literally, "though not all" – which leaves the meaning ambiguous to the hearers. He may mean only that they are literally still not all clean, but the context shows His real intent was to prepare them for His startling announcement in verse 21.

JOHN 13:16 ***a slave is not greater than his master.*** If the master serves, how much more should the servants do so?

a messenger. This is the same word as "apostle," which only occurs here in this Gospel. An apostle was a person sent with the authority to represent the one who sent him. Jesus' followers are to represent His servanthood to others.

notes

notes

Session 6

Surrendering Status

Prepare for the Session

	READINGS	REFLECTIVE QUESTIONS
Monday	Luke 14:7-9	How do you react when you suffer a public humiliation? What have you learned about yourself in such situations?
Tuesday	Luke 14:12-14	When have you done a kindness for someone, knowing the recipient couldn't pay you back?
Wednesday	Matthew 23:1-5	What have you found yourself doing just so people could see you doing it and be impressed? How important is it to you to impress others?
Thursday	Matthew 23:1-7	What indications of status and prestige are important to you? In what way does such status motivate you?
Friday	James 2:1-4	Are you showing favoritism to people considered to have status in the secular world? Whom are you neglecting as a result?
Saturday	James 2:5-9	What are some ways you can show love to people who have no status?
Sunday	Luke 22:28-30	Will there be such a thing as status in the kingdom of heaven? Do you feel motivated to achieve such status?

OUR GOALS FOR THIS SESSION ARE:

BIBLE STUDY

- To see that being a servant leader sometimes requires surrendering human prestige
- To understand that true honor and prestige comes from God alone
- To appreciate how serving the most needy of our world is the best way to serve God

LIFE CHANGE

- To take a group of people to where the homeless hang out and share some food with them
- To sit with the lowest-ranking workers during lunch at work
- At your next social function to avoid totally any reference to whatever might give us prestige

Icebreaker

10-15 minutes

GATHERING THE PEOPLE:

Form horseshoe groups of 6-8.

Status Symbols. Depending on time, choose one or two questions, or answer all three. Go around the group on question 1 and let everyone share. Then go around again on question 2.

1. Which of the following did you consider to be an important status symbol when you were in high school?

☐ Designer clothing
☐ A letterman's jacket
☐ Driving a car to school
☐ Driving a *sports* car to school
☐ Diamond studs in ear or body piercings
☐ other: ____________________

2. When it came to having status in high school, where were you on the social ladder?

☐ The very top
☐ Among the upper rungs
☐ Lost in the middle
☐ The lowest rung
☐ Just above the druggies and the drop-outs

3. Finish this sentence: "The time when I felt I had the greatest status among my peers was when ...

Bible Study

30-45 minutes

The Scripture for this week:

LEARNING FROM THE BIBLE

LUKE 14:7-14

[7]He told a parable to those who were invited, when He noticed
how they would choose the best places for themselves: [8]"When you
are invited by someone to a wedding banquet, don't recline at the
best place, because a more distinguished person than you may have
been invited by your host. [9]The one who invited both of you may
come and say to you, 'Give your place to this man,' and then in
humiliation, you will proceed to take the lowest place.
[10]"But when you are invited, go and recline in the lowest place,
so that when the one who invited you comes, he will say to you,
'Friend, move up higher.' You will then be honored in the presence of
all the other guests. [11]For everyone who exalts himself will be hum-
bled, and the one who humbles himself will be exalted."
[12]He also said to the one who had invited Him, "When you give
a lunch or a dinner, don't invite your friends, your brothers, your rel-
atives, or your rich neighbors, because they might invite you back,
and you would be repaid. [13]On the contrary, when you host a ban-
quet, invite those who are poor, maimed, lame, or blind. [14]And you
will be blessed, because they cannot repay you; for you will be repaid
at the resurrection of the righteous."

...about today's session

A WORD FROM THE LEADER

Write your answers here.

1. Why did Jesus find it important to tell the story about where to sit at a wedding banquet?

2. Why is it significant that this event occurred on a Sabbath day?

3. Why is the person who simply sits in the less prestigious seat in order to get promoted not really "getting" this story?

Identifying with the Story

In horseshoe groups of 6–8, explore questions as time allows.

1. When you were a child and your parent(s) had a dinner party, where did you end up sitting?

   - ☐ At the same table with the grown-ups
   - ☐ At a "child's table" in the same room
   - ☐ At a "child's table" in some other room, away from the adults
   - ☐ At a TV tray, watching the television
   - ☐ In my room
   - ☐ Any place where my parents didn't have to deal with me

2. When did you first get to move up to the "adult's table"? How did you feel about this transition?

3. When in your life have you found yourself being "put in your place" when you had been seeking prestige? How did you respond?

today's session

What is God teaching you from this story?

1. What is to be the main purpose of our lives? How can going after our own honor affect that purpose?

2. In the parable that Jesus told, who was like the host of the banquet and who was like the person who sat first in the most honored seat?

3. What passage from Proverbs teaches something very similar to this parable of Jesus?

4. What are two prerequisites for receiving honor from God?

____

____

5. Of what reality would people have been aware when Jesus was telling them that they should invite the poor, maimed, lame, and blind to their banquets?

Learning from the Story

In horseshoe groups of 6–8, choose an answer and explain why you chose what you did.

1. What indication of your status would you have the hardest time giving up?

- ☐ My parking place at work
- ☐ My title
- ☐ My place on the office letterhead
- ☐ Where my office is located
- ☐ A title I have at church or in a volunteer organization
- ☐ *What* indication of status?
- ☐ other: ______________________________

6

2. In all honesty, what role does human prestige and status play in your motivations right now? Mark your response on the scale below:

1 · · · 2 · · · 3 · · · 4 · · · 5 · · · 6 · · · 7 · · · 8 · · · 9 · · · 10
It means nothing. **It means everything.**

3. Of the things taught in this passage, which would be the hardest for you to do?

- ☐ Voluntarily taking a less prestigious seat
- ☐ Accepting a publicly announced demotion
- ☐ Doing anything to humble myself
- ☐ Inviting needy people to a dinner
- ☐ Giving to someone who has no ability to give back to me

life change lessons

How can you apply this session to your life?

Write your answers here.

1. Why is Francis of Assisi a good example of what it means to forgo human prestige to be a servant leader?

2. Do you agree that seeking status can be an addiction? Where have you seen this being a problem?

____

____

Caring Time

15-20 minutes

CARING TIME

Remain in horseshoe groups of 6-8.

This is the time to develop and express your caring for each other. Start by having group members respond to this question:

"How can the group pray for you in your efforts to apply this week's lesson?"

Include these needs and concerns in your prayer, and then pray about the concerns on the Prayer/ Praise Report. Include prayer for the empty chair.

If you would like to pray silently, say "Amen" when you have finished your prayer, so that the next person will know when to start.

BIBLE STUDY NOTES

Reference Notes

Use these notes to gain further understanding of the text as you study on your own.

LUKE 14:7

the best places. The best places were the seats nearest the hosts. The scene envisioned here is that of the embarrassment experienced by someone who assumed he or she should be in a place of honor, and took that position apart from the host's invitation. When the guest for whom the host had reserved the spot arrived, the presumptuous guest would be humiliated by having to give up the seat.

LUKE 14:8

a wedding banquet. Today those planning a wedding banquet will often take great care establishing a seating chart. Where will the family members of the bride and groom sit in relation to the bride and groom? Where will people be seated who don't get along with each other? What about any ex-spouses or step-relations? All of this is carefully attended to. It would not have been much different in Jesus' time. A person who sat where they were not invited to sit would be inviting trouble.

LUKE 14:11

For everyone who exalts himself will be humbled ... This phrase is repeated in a variety of settings in the New Testament (see Matt. 23:12; Luke 18:14). It gives us what the essence of this parable is about – living a lifestyle of humility.

LUKE 14:12

and you would be repaid. Jesus had been talking about not looking for what one can do to benefit self. In the earlier section He referred to not thinking primarily of the benefit of one's own honor. Now He looked at not thinking of what will benefit us materially. Giving should be out of love. The Greek word for God's kind of love is *agape*, which means love that is selfless, and not seeking a material benefit. Christ did not say that one should never socialize with friends and relatives. Rather He said that if we want to do something truly loving for someone, we should not do it for someone who can return the favor, but for someone who cannot. This indicts much of our Christmas giving, which is often gauged on what the other person is most likely going to give us.

LUKE 14:14

you will be repaid at the resurrection of the righteous. While some may see this as just another kind of self-focused motivation, the point is that we are to have faith that the reward we will receive will be given by God, and that we don't need a material reward in the immediate moment.

notes

Session 7

Surrendering Selfish Ambition

Prepare for the Session

	READINGS	REFLECTIVE QUESTIONS
Monday	James 3:13	Are you able to stay humble when you do good deeds?
Tuesday	James 3:14-16	Who are you feeling envious of right now? How is this envy affecting your ability to serve God?
Wednesday	James 3:17-18	What is being "harvested" from what you have been doing in your life over the last year? Who is benefiting from this harvest besides yourself?
Thursday	Matthew 20:20-23	Are you channeling your own selfish ambitions through another family member, like a spouse, son, or daughter? Are your ambitions in their best interest?
Friday	Matthew 20:24-28	How are your ambitions affecting relationships with coworkers or fellow church members?
Saturday	Acts 8:9-13	Have you ever had the ambition to be "someone great"? How does your faith affect your ambitions?
Sunday	Acts 8:18-24	What do you need to do to make sure your "heart is right" before God, especially in relation to your ambitions?

OUR GOALS FOR THIS SESSION ARE:

BIBLE STUDY

- To learn to differentiate selfish ambition from the healthy ambition God gives us that we might be all He created us to be
- To understand how selfish ambition hurts relationships and keeps us from being good servant leaders
- To see how selfish ambition puts us in the place where God alone belongs in our lives

LIFE CHANGE

- To do something to affirm one we consider to be a rival
- To go to God in prayer each morning this week to submit the day to the glory of God
- To redefine our ambition in terms of serving others

Icebreaker

10-15 minutes

GATHERING THE PEOPLE:

Form horseshoe groups of 6-8.

Childhood Ambitions. Depending on time, choose one or two questions, or answer all three. Go around the group on question 1 and let everyone share. Then go around again on question 2.

1. When you were in junior high, what did you most want to be when you grew up?

   ☐ A famous sports figure
   ☐ What my same-sex parent was
   ☐ A singer or musician
   ☐ Somebody rich
   ☐ A teacher
   ☐ A police officer or fire fighter
   ☐ An airplane pilot
   ☐ An artist or writer
   ☐ The President or an influential politician
   ☐ other: ________________________________

2. What person in your area of ambition (question 1) did you most look up to?

3. If you have given up on your ambition, when do you remember coming to the point where you realized it wasn't going to happen? If you have achieved this ambition, or still hope to, how have your feelings about this ambition changed?

Bible Study

30-45 minutes

The Scripture for this week:

LEARNING FROM THE BIBLE

JAMES 3:13-18

[13]Who is wise and understanding among you? He should show
his works by good conduct with wisdom's gentleness. [14]But if you have
bitter envy and selfish ambition in your heart, don't brag and lie in
defiance of the truth. [15]Such wisdom does not come down from above,
but is earthly, sensual, demonic. [16]For where envy and selfish ambi-
tion exist, there is disorder and every kind of evil. [17]But the wisdom
from above is first pure, then peace-loving, gentle, compliant, full of
mercy and good-fruits, without favoritism and hypocrisy. [18]And the
fruit of righteousness is sown in peace by those who make peace.

...about today's session

A WORD FROM THE LEADER

Write your answers here.

1. What does it mean to be a successful apprentice to Jesus Christ?

2. What is one thing apprentices to Jesus Christ have in common with those who are apprentices to Donald Trump?

ABOUT TODAY'S SESSION (cont'd)

3. Name three biblical examples where people found out that selfish ambition was not the way of Christ:

___

___

___

Identifying with the Story

In horseshoe groups of 6–8, explore questions as time allows.

1. In what area of your life do you most tend to envy others?
   - ☐ Material possessions – I can't help but want what a lot of other people have.
   - ☐ Professional achievement – others have gone so much further than I have.
   - ☐ Family life – other families seem closer and just don't have the problems we have.
   - ☐ Creative talent – I have the desire to create, but not the ability.
   - ☐ Physical appearance – I wish I looked like one of those models or movie stars.

2. When it comes to being ambitious, where would you place yourself on the following scale?

   1 · · · 2 · · · 3 · · · 4 · · · 5 · · · 6 · · · 7 · · · 8 · · · 9 · · · 10

   Another Homer Simpson. **Move over, Bill Gates!**

3. Finish this sentence: "The time when my ambition really got me into trouble was when ..."

today's session

What is God teaching you from this story?

1. What are two examples of how something good can have a bad effect if taken to excess?

___

___

2. What are four symptoms that occur when ambition becomes selfish and unhealthy?

____

____

____

____

3. Why does healthy ambition require that we see things clearly?

4. What great church father spoke of the disruption which occurs when God is not at the center of our lives? What did he say about this?

5. How does ambition that is guided by wisdom from God actually build relationships?

7

Learning from the Story

In horseshoe groups of 6–8, choose an answer and explain why you chose what you did.

1. If Christ as the Great Physician were to give you a check-up on the healthiness of your ambition right now, what do you think would be His conclusion or recommendation?

- ☐ Immediate spiritual "intensive care"
- ☐ Advice that my ego "lose a little weight"
- ☐ That I "give a rest" to all my striving
- ☐ A diet of Scripture and prayer
- ☐ That I stop being a spiritual "couch potato" and *do* something
- ☐ That I am "healthy as a horse" right now
- ☐ other: ______________________________

LEARNING FROM THE STORY (cont'd)

2. What is the main thing you need to do to turn away from selfish ambition and toward a healthier style?
   - ☐ Stop envying certain higher-ups at work
   - ☐ Focus more on doing and less on bragging about what I've done
   - ☐ Make my ambitions subject to prayer and direction by God
   - ☐ Focus more on the needs of others
   - ☐ Build my relational skills
   - ☐ other: ______________________________

3. Finish this sentence: "As I see it right now, letting God direct my ambition would change my life by ..."

life change lessons

How can you apply this session to your life?

Write your answers here.

1. According to an earlier passage in James, what is like looking in a mirror and forgetting what you look like?

2. What should a Christian do to bring out his or her best?

Caring Time

15-20 minutes

CARING TIME

Remain in horseshoe groups of 6-8.

This is the time to develop and express your caring for each other. Start by having group members respond to this question:

"In what way are you seeking peace right now, in your relationships or within your own heart? How can this group help?"

Include these needs and concerns in your prayer, and then pray about the concerns on the Prayer/ Praise Report. Include prayer for the empty chair.

If you would like to pray silently, say "Amen" when you have finished your prayer, so that the next person will know when to start.

BIBLE STUDY NOTES

Reference Notes

Use these notes to gain further understanding of the text as you study on your own.

JAMES 3:13

by good conduct. James' emphasis throughout his letter was on acting on what you believe. See also 2:14-26.

JAMES 3:14

bitter envy. The word translated "bitter" is the same word used in verse 12 to describe brackish water unfit for human consumption. It is now applied to zeal (the word translated "envy" is *zelos*, or "zeal"). Zeal that has gone astray becomes jealousy.
In your heart. This is the issue. What lies at the core of a person's being?
don't brag and lie in defiance of the truth. Those whose hearts are filled with this sense of rivalry and party spirit ought not pretend that they are speaking God's wisdom. To do this is merely to compound the wrong that is taking place.

JAMES 3:15

earthly, sensual, demonic. Note the progression from the mildly negative ("earthly") to the strongly negative ("demonic.") Ambition, which is to lift us up to a higher plane, drags us down to the lowest levels when it is selfish.

JAMES 3:17

Hellenistic teachers of rhetoric and ethics had their pupils memorize lists of virtues and vices as part of their moral instruction. This list is probably influenced by that practice.
peace-loving. This is the opposite of envy and selfish ambition. True wisdom produces right relationships between people, which is the root idea behind the word "peace" when it is used in the New Testament.
compliant. True wisdom is willing to listen, then yield when persuaded.
full of mercy and good-fruits. True wisdom reaches out to the unfortunate in practical ways, a point James never tires of making.
without favoritism James had already written of how favoritism compromises the command we have from Christ to love our neighbor (2:1-13).
or hypocrisy. True wisdom does not act or pretend. It is honest, sincere, and genuine.

JAMES 3:18

... those who make peace. James frequently echoed the moral teachings of Jesus, particularly those in the Sermon on the Mount. Here there are echoes of "Blessed are the peacemakers."

notes

Session

8

A Passionate Servant

Prepare for the Session

	READINGS	REFLECTIVE QUESTIONS
Monday	Luke 7:36-38	How are you showing your gratitude for all that Christ has done for you?
Tuesday	Luke 7:41-43	If you could put a monetary value on all that God has done for you, what value would it be? What would the value be of what He has done for you just in the past month?
Wednesday	Luke 7:44-48	What "many sins" can you think of that God has forgiven you for in the past month? Has God's forgiveness ever moved you to tears?
Thursday	2 Samuel 6:14-16	When have you been full of such joy before God that you couldn't keep yourself from dancing? How did people who didn't understand your joy react?
Friday	2 Samuel 6:20-22	Is it okay to celebrate something so passionately that you end up looking like a fool to others? Has this ever happened to you? How did you react?
Saturday	Matthew 22:37	Are you truly loving God with your whole self?
Sunday	1 Peter 1:8-9	Has your faith brought you the joy that Peter wrote about? Why or why not?

OUR GOALS FOR THIS SESSION ARE:

BIBLE STUDY

- To understand that the feeling we have about the serving we do does make a difference
- To consider what it means to serve God with passion
- To point to the forgiveness God has shown us in Jesus Christ as the main motivator we have for serving

LIFE CHANGE

- To focus our prayer this week on asking God to renew our hearts for service
- To evaluate our motivation for each job we are asked to take on
- To lay our tears at the feet of Christ

Icebreaker

10-15 minutes

GATHERING THE PEOPLE:

Form horseshoe groups of 6-8.

The Tracks of Our Tears. Depending on time, choose one or two questions, or answer all three. Go around the group on question 1 and let everyone share. Then go around again on question 2.

1. What was taught about crying in the family in which you were raised?

   - ☐ Big boys/girls don't cry.
   - ☐ Tears are a good way to get what you want sometimes.
   - ☐ Tears are nothing to be ashamed of.
   - ☐ Sharing tears is a great bonding experience.
   - ☐ Tears mean the other person wins.
   - ☐ Tears are the rule in life; smiles are the exception.
   - ☐ other: ____________________

2. When as a child or adolescent do you remember feeling close to someone because you cried together?

3. What is most likely to bring you to tears as an adult?

- ☐ A sad song or movie
- ☐ Soap operas
- ☐ A moving worship experience
- ☐ Family conflict
- ☐ Personal depression
- ☐ Professional frustration
- ☐ A sweet act of caring by a loved one
- ☐ A disappointing loss by a sports team
- ☐ other: ______________________________

Bible Study

30-45 minutes

The Scripture for this week:

LEARNING FROM THE BIBLE

LUKE 7:36-50

[36]Then one of the Pharisees invited Him to eat with him. He
entered the Pharisee's house and reclined at the table. [37]And a woman
in the town who was a sinner found out that Jesus was reclining at
the table in the Pharisee's house. She brought an alabaster flask of
fragrant oil [38]and stood behind Him at His feet, weeping, and began
to wash His feet with her tears. She wiped His feet with the hair of
her head, kissing them and anointing them with the fragrant oil.
[39]When the Pharisee who had invited Him saw this, he said to
himself, "This man, if He were a prophet, would know who and what
kind of woman this is who is touching Him—that she's a sinner!"
[40]Jesus replied to him, "Simon, I have something to say to you."
"Teacher," he said, "say it."
[41]"A creditor had two debtors. One owed 500 denarii, and the
other 50. [42]Since they could not pay it back, he graciously forgave
them both. So, which of them will love him more?"
[43]Simon answered, "I suppose the one he forgave more."
"You have judged correctly," He told him. [44]Turning to the woman,
He said to Simon, "Do you see this woman? I entered your house;
you gave Me no water for My feet, but she, with her tears, has
washed My feet and wiped them with her hair. [45]You gave Me no kiss,
but she hasn't stopped kissing My feet since I came in. [46]You didn't
anoint My head with oil, but she has anointed My feet with fragrant
oil. [47]Therefore I tell you, her many sins have been forgiven; that's
why she loved much. But the one who is forgiven little, loves little."
[48]Then He said to her, "Your sins are forgiven."

BIBLE STUDY (cont'd)

[49] *Those who were at the table with Him began to say among themselves, "Who is this man who even forgives sins?"*

[50] *And He said to the woman, "Your faith has saved you. Go in peace."*

...about today's session

A WORD FROM THE LEADER

Write your answers here.

1. What does it mean to do something "with passion"?

2. What does it mean that the woman in this story was "a sinner"?

3. What does *not* change about this woman after she encounters Christ?

Identifying with the Story

In horseshoe groups of 6–8, explore questions as time allows.

1. When in your life have you known someone who looked down on you or spoke of you like Simon spoke of this woman?
   - ☐ When I was a "screw-up" in high school or college
   - ☐ When I went through divorce or bankruptcy
   - ☐ When I was dating someone from a higher socioeconomic level and met his/her family
   - ☐ Every time I have had to be with my in-laws
   - ☐ Never
   - ☐ other: ______________________________

2. When do you remember feeling as sorrowful for what you had done as this woman seems to feel? How did you express those feelings?

3. Which of the following do you feel most passionate about at this point in your life?

- ▢ My profession
- ▢ My family
- ▢ My country
- ▢ My faith
- ▢ Sports
- ▢ Politics
- ▢ Music or the arts
- ▢ other: ______________________

today's session

What is God teaching you from this story?

1. What did it mean when a host did not provide for the washing of a guest's feet?

2. What three acts of service did this woman perform for Jesus?

____

____

____

3. What does Jesus say that makes it seem He had already forgiven her before the events of this story?

8

4. Who were two persons in biblical stories who served more out of a sense of obligation and duty than passionate love?

____

____

5. How is the woman in this story and the way she serves different than the persons referred to in our previous question?

Learning from the Story

⊃ In horseshoe groups of 6–8, choose an answer and explain why you chose what you did.

1. Which of the things that this woman did would have been hardest for you to do?
   - ☐ Going into the home of someone who despised me
   - ☐ Washing someone's dirty feet
   - ☐ Crying in front of other people—especially enemies
   - ☐ Touching someone I was not related to
   - ☐ other: ______________________________

2. If you were to put yourself into the parable Jesus told here, would you be closer to the one who had been forgiven 50 denarii or the one who had been forgiven 500 denarii? How does this affect your love for God?

3. If you were to have the passion and love of this woman, how would it change the way you are serving right now?

life change lessons

How can you apply this session to your life?

Write your answers here.

1. What are three spurious motivations for serving?

   ____

   ____

   ____

2. What are two appropriate motivations for serving in the name of Christ?

   ____

   ____

Caring Time

15-20 minutes

CARING TIME

Remain in horseshoe groups of 6-8.

This is the time to develop and express your caring for each other. Start by having group members respond to these questions:

"What are you feeling a need to be forgiven of right now? How can this group be in prayer for this need?"

Include these needs and concerns in your prayer, and then pray about the concerns on the Prayer/ Praise Report. Include prayer for the empty chair.

If you would like to pray silently, say "Amen" when you have finished your prayer, so that the next person will know when to start.

Reference Notes

BIBLE STUDY NOTES

Use these notes to gain further understanding of the text as you study on your own.

LUKE 7:36

one of the Pharisees. Why Simon (v. 40) invited Jesus is unclear. His lack of provision to his guest of some of the common courtesies of the day (vv. 44-46) indicates his opinion of Jesus probably was not especially high. Still, he would not have eaten with Jesus at all if he considered Jesus to be a "sinner," for the Pharisees prided themselves in not associating with "sinners."

reclined at the table. People ate while reclining on their left side on low couches arranged around a table, such that their feet would be stretched out behind them.

LUKE 7:37

who was a sinner. While not stated, probably a life of sexual immorality is meant. The woman, who was certainly not an invited guest, may simply have joined other people in Simon's courtyard who had gathered to listen to Jesus talk. Although there is no biblical evidence, some identified this sinful woman with Mary Magdalene (tradition said that she had been a prostitute). Since Mary Magdalene was one of the women who provided financially for Jesus out of her own funds (8:1-3) and since it is unlikely that Jesus would allow His ministry to be funded by money tainted by prostitution, this tradition is suspect.

LUKE 7:38

This verse is loaded with emotion. The woman's tears show her extreme conviction of her sin, as she stood by the feet of Jesus. For a woman to loose her hair in public was scandalous; using it to dry her tears from

REFERENCE NOTES LUKE 7:38 (cont'd)	Jesus' feet marked her great humility before Him. Normally a person's head would be anointed as a sign of honor. (The Hebrew word *Messiah* means "anointed one.") Like John the Baptist, who felt unworthy to undo the thongs of the Messiah's sandals (3:16), perhaps this woman felt she was so unworthy that she dare only anoint Jesus' feet. That Jesus accepted these acts shows much about His character. He did not let what people might think dictate how He related to people. He saw her love and penitence, and responded to that instead of to public opinion.
LUKE 7:39	Simon the Pharisee, seeing only that Jesus violated the acceptable religious and social code by allowing such a woman to touch Him like this, saw nothing of her repentance or gratitude.
LUKE 7:41-43	***500 denarii ... 50.*** The difference here is between owing what one could earn in 18 months versus owing what could be earned in less than two months. Then, as now, it would be the rare moneylender who would cancel either debt! Part of what Jesus was saying was that God cancels debts (in the form of sins) that are far greater than what most humans would cancel. A similar point is made in the Parable of the Unmerciful Servant, where the amount the Master forgave was greater still (Matt. 18: 23-35). Simon rightly got the point that the man with the greatest debt would be most grateful.
LUKE 7:44-46	While Simon had not behaved discourteously to Jesus as his guest, he had performed none of the special acts of hospitality that were customary for important guests. By contrast, this woman, who owed nothing to Jesus from a social point of view, showed her love and respect for Him by cleansing His feet, welcoming Him with her kisses, and anointing Him with expensive perfume.
LUKE 7:47	Jesus was not saying that the woman was forgiven because she had shown such extravagant love, just as the debt was not cancelled because of any act on the part of the debtor (v. 42). Rather her love expressed her gratitude for the forgiveness she had received.
LUKE 7:47	***Your faith has saved you.*** It is trusting oneself to Jesus that leads to salvation from the penalty and power of sin. ***go in peace.*** This was a common saying, but on the lips of Jesus it was uttered not simply as a wish but as an expression of fact.

notes

notes

Session

9

A Trusting Servant

Prepare for the Session

	READINGS	REFLECTIVE QUESTIONS
Monday	Luke 1:26-28	In what ways have you sensed that "the Lord is with you" in the past few weeks? How might this awareness affect how you serve Him in the weeks to come?
Tuesday	Luke 1:29-30	What have you been afraid that God might ask you to do? What do you think God might do to reassure you in the midst of your fear?
Wednesday	Luke 1:31-37	What might you attempt if you truly believed in your heart that nothing is impossible with God?
Thursday	Psalm 31:1-6	When you face difficult times, do you trust God or your own abilities?
Friday	Psalm 37:3-6	How does your trust in God show in your behavior?
Saturday	Psalm 40:1-4	In what ways are you expressing to God your thanksgiving for His trust-worthiness?
Sunday	Genesis 22:1-14	How difficult is it for you to trust God's provision when it is not immediately obvious how a need will be provided for?

OUR GOALS FOR THIS SESSION ARE:

BIBLE STUDY

- To appreciate the role of trust in being a good servant leader
- To see that when we trust God, nothing God wants to happen will be impossible
- To point to Mary, the mother of Jesus, as a good example of what it means to trust the promises of God

LIFE CHANGE

- To post the promise, "For nothing will be impossible with God," somewhere we will see it regularly
- To participate in trust falls with our family or close friends
- To try something for God that we previously have been a little scared to try

Icebreaker

10-15 minutes

GATHERING THE PEOPLE:

Form horseshoe groups of 6-8.

Promises, promises! Depending on time, choose one or two questions, or answer all three. Go around the group on question 1 and let everyone share. Then go around again on question 2.

1. What was the attitude toward promises in the family in which you were raised? Mark the scale below:

   1 · · · 2 · · · 3 · · · 4 · · · 5 · · · 6 · · · 7 · · · 8 · · · 9 · · · 10

   Promises are made to be broken. — **A person's word is sacred.**

2. During the course of your life, what kind of promises have you become *most* suspicious of?

   ☐ Promises of romantic love
   ☐ Promises made by persons running for office
   ☐ Promises made by teenagers
   ☐ Promises made in commercial advertising
   ☐ Promises I make to myself to change
   ☐ other: ____________________

3. Finish this sentence: "The time I remember someone really coming through on a promise to me was when ..."

Bible Study

30-45 minutes

The Scripture for this week:

LEARNING FROM THE BIBLE

LUKE 1:26-38

26In the sixth month, the angel Gabriel was sent by God to a town
in Galilee called Nazareth, 27to a virgin engaged to a man named
Joseph, of the house of David. The virgin's name was Mary. 28And he
came to her and said, "Rejoice, favored woman! The Lord is with you."
29But she was deeply troubled by this statement and was wondering
what kind of greeting this could be. 30 Then the angel told her:

Do not be afraid, Mary, for you have found favor with God.
31Now listen: You will conceive and give birth to a son,
and you will call His name JESUS.
32He will be great
and will be called the Son of the Most High,
and the Lord God will give Him the throne of His father David.
33He will reign over the house of Jacob forever,
and His kingdom will have no end.

34Mary asked the angel, "How can this be, since I have not been
intimate with a man?"

35The angel replied to her:

The Holy Spirit will come upon you,
and the power of the Most High will overshadow you.
Therefore the holy child to be born
will be called the Son of God.

36And consider Elizabeth your relative—even she has conceived
a son in her old age, and this is the sixth month for her who was
called barren. 37For nothing will be impossible with God."

38"Consider me the Lord's slave," said Mary. "May it be done to
me according to your word." Then the angel left her.

...about today's session

A WORD FROM THE LEADER

Write your answers here.

1. At about what age were young women married in New Testament times?

2. What examples are given of people who did not entirely trust a promise God gave them?

 ____

 ____

 ____

3. How was Mary's reaction different from the ones referred to in the previous question?

Identifying with the Story

In horseshoe groups of 6–8, explore questions as time allows.

1. What is the closest you have come to having someone make an announcement to you with the emotional impact of what Mary heard from the angel?

 ☐ When the doctor told me about "the lump"
 ☐ When my spouse proposed
 ☐ When we heard we were pregnant
 ☐ When I heard I had been laid off
 ☐ When I was selected for an honor I never expected to receive
 ☐ other: ______________________________

2. What would you say is the closest thing to a miracle that God has brought into your life?

3. Whom do you trust?

 ☐ Only one or two of my closest friends
 ☐ My family and a variety of friends
 ☐ Most people, once I get to know them
 ☐ other: ______________________________
 ☐ Nobody
 ☐ God alone

today's session

What is God teaching you from this story?

1. Why could inability to trust be considered a "disability"?

2. What four life situations are mentioned where we need to trust others?

   ____

   ____

   ____

   ____

3. What are four things Mary could have feared?

   ____

   ____

   ____

   ____

4. What are three other New Testament situations where we are told that with God all things are possible?

   ____

   ____

   ____

5. What did Mary say that indicated her trust and submission to God?

Learning from the Story

In horseshoe groups of 6–8, choose an answer and explain why you chose what you did.

1. Had you been Mary, what would you have been most afraid of?
   - ☐ Talking to an angel
   - ☐ Having to talk to Joseph
   - ☐ What people thought
   - ☐ The physical process of having a baby in those times
   - ☐ The responsibility involved in having to raise the Son of God
   - ☐ other: ______________________________

2. Mary asked a question for clarification before she affirmed her trust in God's promise. If you could ask "a clarification question" of God right now, what would it be?

3. What will be the hardest thing for you to trust in the way God is calling you to trust?
   - ☐ Overcoming a life pattern of distrust
   - ☐ Learning exactly what it is God promises me
   - ☐ Submitting when I am used to being in control
   - ☐ Maintaining my resolve to do so
   - ☐ other: ______________________________

life change lessons

How can you apply this session to your life?

Write your answers here.

1. What are some examples of the kind of life experiences that shape how easy or how difficult it is for us to trust?

   ____

   ____

   ____

2. How can an exercise like a "trust fall" help a person learn to trust?

Caring Time

15-20 minutes

CARING TIME

Remain in horseshoe groups of 6-8.

This is the time to develop and express your caring for each other. Start by having group members respond to this question:

"What 'impossible' challenge are you facing in the weeks to come that this group can support you with in prayer?"

Include these needs and concerns in your prayer, and then pray about the concerns on the Prayer/ Praise Report. Include prayer for the empty chair.

If you would like to pray silently, say "Amen" when you have finished your prayer, so that the next person will know when to start.

Reference Notes

BIBLE STUDY NOTES

Use these notes to gain further understanding of the text as you study on your own.

LUKE 1:26

In the sixth month. This refers to the sixth month of Elizabeth's pregnancy.
a town in Galilee called Nazareth. Nazareth was an insignificant little village (John 1:46) in the province of Galilee. God often uses what others see as small or insignificant, as with the "little town of Bethlehem."

LUKE 1:27

a virgin engaged to a man. Betrothal, usually lasting for about a year, could occur when a girl was as young as 12 years old. This was a far more binding arrangement than engagements today. Although sexual relations were not permitted, the woman had the legal status of a wife, and the relationship could only be broken by divorce. The virgin birth of Jesus, although only mentioned in Matthew and Luke in the entire New Testament, traces its roots to the prophecy of the child spoken of in Isaiah 7:14.
named Joseph, of the house of David. The Messiah was to come through the line of David, the most famous king of Israel's history (2 Sam. 7:16; Ps. 132:11).

LUKE 1:28

The Lord is with you. This phrase is often used as a statement of God's special intention to equip a person for His service (Josh. 1:5; Judg. 6:12; Matt. 28:20).

REFERENCE NOTES (cont'd)

LUKE 1:32 ***He will be great ... the Son of the Most High.*** Jesus, like John the Baptist (v. 15), would be considered "great," but the greatness of these two men would be of different orders. John would be great "in the sight of the Lord" (v. 15) as "a prophet of the Most High" (v. 76), but Jesus' greatness consists of His being the Son of the Most High (God).

LUKE 1:34 ***How can this be ...?*** Zechariah asked this question of the angel when informed that he and his wife Elizabeth would have a child (v. 18.) He asked out of doubt that such a thing could come to pass, since Elizabeth was quite old. Mary, however, did not register doubt as much as wonder.

LUKE 1:37 ***nothing will be impossible with God.*** The ultimate ground for Mary's faith rested on this fact. In similar circumstances, when Sarah laughed at the idea that a woman her age could have a child, God said, "Is anything too hard for the Lord?" (Gen. 18:14.) This conviction gave courage and faith in the hardest times (Jer. 32:27.) Jesus emphasized this belief in the impossible on several occasions (Matt. 17:20; Mark 9:23; 10:27).

notes

notes

Session

10

A Watchful Servant

Prepare for the Session

	READINGS	REFLECTIVE QUESTIONS
Monday	Matthew 24:42-44	If Christ returned today, would you welcome His arrival?
Tuesday	Matthew 24:45-47	If you gave a report of your stewartship to Christ, what would you use show your faithfulness?
Wednesday	Matthew 24:48-51	What "fellow slaves" might have complaints against you? Would their complaints be justified?
Thursday	Matthew 25:1-5	How have you been impatient with God's timetable? How can you improve your ability to wait on God's timing?
Friday	Matthew 25:6-9	Do you expect others to rescue you from your own irresponsibility? How can you better take responsibility for yourself?
Saturday	Matthew 25:10-13	What doors to ministry have closed to you because you weren't prepared? How can you keep this from happening again?
Sunday	Ezekiel 33:1-6	What is your responsibility to be watchful on the behalf of others? How well are you doing in helping others to be watchful for themselves?

OUR GOALS FOR THIS SESSION ARE:

BIBLE STUDY

- To explore what it means to live a life watchful of our Master's return
- To better appreciate how caring for those around us is part of what we must do until Christ returns
- To understand that living a responsible personal life is also part of being servant leaders

LIFE CHANGE

- To read of some of the biblical signs of Christ's return
- To find one new way to "feed" our fellow servants
- To commit to doing nothing in private this week that we would not want fully revealed in public

Icebreaker

10-15 minutes

GATHERING THE PEOPLE:

Form horseshoe groups of 6-8.

Taken by Surprise. Depending on time, choose one or two questions, or answer all three. Go around the group on question 1 and let everyone share. Then go around again on question 2.

1. Which of the following most took you by surprise?

- ☐ My spouse's proposal
- ☐ One of our pregnancies
- ☐ Middle age
- ☐ My draft notice
- ☐ Falling in love
- ☐ My child finally growing up
- ☐ A "pink slip"
- ☐ A doctor's discouraging report
- ☐ My invitation to the AARP

2. When something takes you by surprise, which of the following are you most likely to do?

- ☐ Stay cool – act like I saw it coming.
- ☐ Panic! – I don't like surprises.
- ☐ After that first jolt, make my adjustments and "go with the flow."
- ☐ Enjoy being surprised! – Life is too predictable anyway.
- ☐ other: ______________________________

3. What do you see ahead of you in your life that you want to make sure does *not* take you by surprise?

Bible Study

30-45 minutes

The Scripture for this week:

LEARNING FROM THE BIBLE

MATTHEW 24:42-51

[42]Therefore be alert, since you don't know what day your Lord is coming. [43]But know this: If the homeowner had known what time the thief was coming, he would have stayed alert and not let his house be broken into. [44]This is why you also should get ready, because the Son of Man is coming at an hour you do not expect.

[45]"Who then is a faithful and sensible slave, whom his master has put in charge of his household, to give them food at the proper time? [46]Blessed is that slave whom his master, when he comes, will find working. [47]I assure you: He will put him in charge of all his possessions. [48]But if that wicked slave says in his heart, 'My master is delayed,' [49]and starts to beat his fellow slaves, and eats and drinks with drunkards, [50]that slave's master will come on a day he does not expect and at a time he does not know. [51]He will cut him to pieces and assign him a place with the hypocrites. In that place there will be weeping and gnashing of teeth.

...about today's session

A WORD FROM THE LEADER

Write your answers here.

1. In the parable Jesus told here, what were two ways that the slave misbehaved when he determined that his master was delayed?

10

2. How did the disciples' react when Jesus first ascended to heaven? What was wrong with this manner of "watching and waiting"?

ABOUT TODAY'S SESSION (cont'd)

3. What are two other biblical examples of those who did a poor job watching and waiting?

____

____

Identifying with the Story

In horseshoe groups of 6–8, explore questions as time allows.

1. What is the worst thing you remember happening when you were a teenager and your parents put you in charge or left you on your own?

2. How did you generally feel about being left in charge when you were a teen?

   - ☐ Proud to be trusted
   - ☐ Worried about what might go wrong
   - ☐ Lonely
   - ☐ Imposed upon
   - ☐ Ready to party!
   - ☐ Who cares?
   - ☐ other: ______________________

3. What is generally your reaction when you are left in charge of something today?

   - ☐ Why does it always have to be me?
   - ☐ I hope I don't mess up like I did as a teenager!
   - ☐ Still, proud to be trusted.
   - ☐ Of course I will be in charge – who else could do it?
   - ☐ This is too much stress!
   - ☐ other: ______________________

today's session

What is God teaching you from this story?

1. Why should we be looking to the second coming of Christ?

2. What else should being alert to Christ include besides looking for the second coming?

3. In the parable, what was the slave put in charge to do? What does this say to us?

4. What are two types of "feeding our fellow servants" we might be called on to do? With both of them mention a biblical example.

____________________ -- example: ____________________.

____________________ -- example: ____________________.

5. What truth do we need to be alert to if we are to keep ourselves from body-destroying personal sins, like alcohol and drug abuse?

Learning from the Story

In horseshoe groups of 6–8, choose an answer and explain why you chose what you did.

1. Which of the following are you likely to do when you think no one is looking?

- ☐ Sneak some extra dessert
- ☐ Drink juice or milk out of the bottle
- ☐ Speed
- ☐ Take office supplies for personal use
- ☐ Pick my nose
- ☐ Eat food that has dropped on the floor
- ☐ Make fun of someone

2. In what ways have you abused those around you recently? How would it have changed things had you been alert to the presence of Christ in the other person?

LEARNING FROM THE STORY (cont'd)

3. What do you need to change about yourself to become more alert and watchful?
   - ☐ I need to remember that Christ will return as judge.
   - ☐ I need to be alert to the fact that what I do to others, I do to Christ.
   - ☐ I need to learn the signs of Christ's return.
   - ☐ I need to be alert to the fact that my body is a member of Christ.

life change lessons

How can you apply this session to your life?

Write your answers here.

1. What is the only true test or standard we have for monitoring our behavior?

2. What do we need to do if we do not see what Scripture says we should be seeing?

Caring Time

15-20 minutes

CARING TIME

Remain in horseshoe groups of 6-8.

This is the time to develop and express your caring for each other. Start by having group members respond to this question:

"With what abusive behavior do you especially need prayer support right now?"

Include these needs and concerns in your prayer, and then pray about the concerns on the Prayer/ Praise Report. Include prayer for the empty chair.

If you would like to pray silently, say "Amen" when you have finished your prayer, so that the next person will know when to start.

Reference Notes

BIBLE STUDY NOTES

Use these notes to gain further understanding of the text as you study on your own.

MATTHEW 24:42

Therefore be alert. Persons who are not alert to what is happening around them will miss God's action in the world and the signs with which He seeks to warn us. In another context Jesus chided the Pharisees for observing the signs of changing weather, while not paying attention to the signs of what God was doing (Matt. 16:1-4).

since you don't know which day your Lord is coming. While one error is to not be alert to the signs of the times, another error is thinking we know when Christ's return will be. Many have attempted to calculate the time of His return, some down to the day and hour, but the point made here is that we do not know. Since we do not know, we need to be all the more vigilant to stay faithful all along.

MATTHEW 24:43

what time the thief was coming. That Christ's return would be like a thief in the night is repeated frequently in the New Testament (1Thess. 5:1-4; 2 Pet. 3:10; Rev. 3:3; 16:15). The point is not that Christ's return is a danger to be guarded against, but rather that it will not be something that is predictable or for which we can prepare at the last minute. It will come as a surprise, ready or not.

MATTHEW 24:45-51

When the master was away, one servant would be appointed as the head of the household. If he abused this position for his own indulgence, the sudden appearance of his master would bring judgment. The point here is that watchfulness is not a matter of scanning the horizon for signs of the Lord's return, but of faithfully fulfilling the responsibilities God has assigned His people.

MATTHEW 24:47

He will put him in charge of all His possessions. Faithfulness is rewarded by giving greater responsibility and with it, higher status. This is similar to the teaching in the Parable of the Talents, where the master tells those who had invested well, "Well done, good and faithful slave! You were faithful over a few things; I will put you in charge of many things ..." (Matt. 25:21).

MATTHEW 24:48

My master is delayed. Early Christians thought that Jesus would come back right away, and were concerned when this did not happen. This parable, along with the Parable of the Ten Virgins, addressed how they were to behave during this "delay." The issue is also addressed in 2 Peter 3:3-16.

MATTHEW 24:51

weeping and gnashing of teeth. In Matthew this is a common phrase, used to describe one's reaction to the torments of hell (see Matt. 8:12; 13:42; 13:50; 22:13; 25:30).

notes

Session

11

Renewed to Serve

Prepare for the Session

	READINGS	REFLECTIVE QUESTIONS
Monday	Luke 10:38	Do you have the gift of hospitality? In what ways might Christ be calling you to minister by welcoming people into your home?
Tuesday	Luke 10:39	How much time are you spending "sitting at Jesus' feet" listening and learning? Is this time adequate?
Wednesday	Luke 10:40	What is the chief cause of your being stressed and distracted right now? How can you entrust these things more into the hands of God?
Thursday	Luke 10:41-42	Are you keeping your life focused on "the one necessary thing"?
Friday	Mark 1:35	Have you found a special place where you can get away for quiet and solitude?
Saturday	Mark 1:36-37	How well are you handling the people who make demands on your time? Are you able to tell them "no" when you need to? Are you able to get away from these demands when you need to?
Sunday	Mark 1:38-39	Is your devotional life keeping you energized and focused on your mission?

OUR GOALS FOR THIS SESSION ARE:

BIBLE STUDY

- To appreciate the importance of servant leaders taking time to listen "at the feet of Christ"
- To consider the need to balance time serving God and others with time to find spiritual renewal ourselves
- To survey various ways modern servant leaders can spend time listening to Christ

LIFE CHANGE

- To develop or expand our private devotional time
- To plan an hour of complete silence to use in meditation
- To use notes in worship to sharpen our listening skills

Icebreaker

10-15 minutes

GATHERING THE PEOPLE:

Form horseshoe groups of 6-8.

A World of Distractions. Depending on time, choose one or two questions, or answer all three. Go around the group on question 1 and let everyone share. Then go around again on question 2.

1. What are you most likely to be distracted by?

☐ Noisy children
☐ An attractive person of the opposite sex
☐ The thought of an unfinished task
☐ A messy room
☐ People who are having fun when I am not
☐ Ticking clocks ... music on the radio ... nearby traffic ... what was the question again?
☐ Nothing distracts me.
☐ other: ________________________________

2. What is a responsibility you have regularly that you so dread that you *look* for something to distract you?

☐ Cleaning house
☐ Balancing the checkbook
☐ Doing the laundry
☐ Taking care of the yard
☐ Making phone calls to resolve conflicts
☐ other: ________________________________

3. Finish this sentence: "The overriding concern that I wish someone could distract me from right now is ..."

Bible Study

30-45 minutes

The Scripture for this week:

LEARNING FROM THE BIBLE

LUKE 10:38-42

[38]While they were traveling, He entered a village, and a woman named Martha welcomed Him into her home. [39]She had a sister named Mary, who also sat at the Lord's feet and was listening to what He said. [40]But Martha was distracted by her many tasks, and she came up and asked, "Lord, don't You care that my sister has left me to serve alone? So tell her to give me a hand."

[41]The Lord answered her, "Martha, Martha, you are worried and upset about many things, [42]but one thing is necessary. Mary has made the right choice, and it will not be taken away from her."

...about today's session

A WORD FROM THE LEADER

Write your answers here.

1. What two negative symptoms often appear when we "run out of gas" spiritually?

____

____

2. How did Martha evidence that she needed a break from serving?

3. How do we know that even Jesus needed time to get away from the pressures of serving others?

Identifying with the Story

In horseshoe groups of 6–8, explore questions as time allows.

1. When there is work to be done in order to host company, is your own personal style more like that of Mary or Martha? Mark your response on the scale below:

   1 · · · 2 · · · 3 · · · 4 · · · 5 · · · 6 · · · 7 · · · 8 · · · 9 · · · 10
   People first like Mary **Work first like Martha**

2. When have you felt like you were left "holding the bag" in regard to some work you thought you were supposed to share with others? What did you do about it?

3. Had you been there with Mary and Martha, what might Jesus have said that you are getting too "worried and upset about" at this stage of your life?

today's session

What is God teaching you from this story?

1. Why is it so hard to slow down when our priority is to please people?

2. What did Jesus say our number one priority should be?

3. What are two needs we can address by taking time to listen to what Christ would say to us?

   ____

   ____

4. What are four important "tools for listening" we should use as we listen at the feet of Christ?

____

____

____

____

5. Taking quiet time helps us to get in touch with what two entities?

____

____

Learning from the Story

In horseshoe groups of 6–8, choose an answer and explain why you chose what you did.

1. Had you been Mary when the conflict in this story occurred, what would you have been most likely to have done?

- ☐ I would have guiltily gotten up and started working.
- ☐ I would have gotten in a shouting match with Martha.
- ☐ I would have ignored Martha, just to bother her.
- ☐ I would have waited for Jesus' judgment, then made my "told ya' so!" face at Martha.
- ☐ I would have made an arrangement with her before things got so messy.
- ☐ I would have held my ground, but tried to sooth Martha's feelings later.

2. When have you found people making demands on you when you were trying to take your time to "sit at the feet of Christ"? How did you respond to those demands? How can you better protect this time?

LEARNING FROM THE STORY (cont'd)

3. What tool(s) do you need to make better use of in your efforts to listen to what Christ would say to you? Mark all that apply:
   - ☐ Prayer
   - ☐ Silence
   - ☐ Individual retreats
   - ☐ Group retreats
   - ☐ Worship
   - ☐ Bible and devotional reading

life change lessons

How can you apply this session to your life?

Write your answers here.

1. In what prophet can we find a reference to how even though we have ears, we don't hear?

2. What does the person need to do who really wants to hear what Christ is saying?

Caring Time

15-20 minutes

CARING TIME

Remain in horseshoe groups of 6-8.

This is the time to develop and express your caring for each other. Start by having group members respond to this question:

"How can this group support you in prayer in your efforts to strengthen your devotional life?"

Include these needs and concerns in your prayer, and then pray about the concerns on the Prayer/ Praise Report. Include prayer for the empty chair.

If you would like to pray silently, say "Amen" when you have finished your prayer, so that the next person will know when to start.

BIBLE STUDY NOTES

Reference Notes

Use these notes to gain further understanding of the text as you study on your own.

LUKE 10:38

village. Bethany, just on the outskirts of Jerusalem, was the home of Martha and Mary, and their brother Lazarus.

a woman named Martha. Martha and Mary also appear in John 11:1-44, where their brother Lazarus died and was raised from the dead by Jesus. In that story Martha, rather than Mary, was more faithful. In today's story, Mary was the faithful one.

Martha welcoming Him into her home. It appears that it was Martha's home (she was the head of the household). That would explain why she would feel more responsible for preparations.

LUKE 10:40

my sister has left me to serve alone. This is a classic clash between a disciplined, task-oriented servant (Martha), and a more impulsive, person-oriented student (Mary). Martha's claim that Mary had left her to do all the work assumes the priority that work always comes first over learning and socialization. None of this is to say that Jesus "sided" against the more task-oriented person. He simply said that in that situation, stopping to spend time with Him was the highest priority, and Mary had chosen that priority.

LUKE 10:41

you are worried and upset. Martha was like the thorny soil in which the fruit is choked by life's worries (8:14).

about many things. Martha's problem was an inability to focus her life around one central priority. Jesus calls us to focus our lives around the central priority of the kingdom of God (Matt. 6:33).

LUKE 10:42

one thing is necessary. Jesus did not say that a simple meal was all that was needed. He did say that listening and responding to Him is the single most critical thing in all of life. Mary had chosen to do that rather than being distracted.

notes

Session 12

Serving a Larger Family

Prepare for the Session

	READINGS	REFLECTIVE QUESTIONS
Monday	Isaiah 49:1-2	What tools has God given you to use in service of Him and others?
Tuesday	Isaiah 49:3-4	How discouraged are you right now as you seek to do what God calls you to do? How can you rely on God to help you with that discouragement?
Wednesday	Isaiah 49:5-6	What bigger task is God challenging you with right now? Are you feeling up to the challenge?
Thursday	Isaiah 49:7	How is God being glorified because of you?
Friday	Acts 16:6-7	In what way has God *limited* the scope of where you were being called to minister? How did God let you know of these limits?
Saturday	Acts 16:8-10	Who might God be using to call you to ministry with a group of people who have been neglected?
Sunday	Acts 10:27-29	How might God be opening your mind to people you previously looked down upon?

OUR GOALS FOR THIS SESSION ARE:

BIBLE STUDY

- To see how Isaiah was challenged to go beyond rescuing the lost of Israel to call Israel to be a light to the nations
- To understand that servant leaders are often called to serve beyond their own little group
- To see how failure can come from taking on too small of a task because we are not challenged to do all God is calling us to do

LIFE CHANGE

- To visit with three people in the community around our church to see what they consider to be the greatest needs of the community
- To develop a friendship with someone of another culture
- To write a letter or e-mail to a mission worker in another country

Icebreaker

10-15 minutes

GATHERING THE PEOPLE:

Form horseshoe groups of 6-8.

Going Nowhere. Depending on time, choose one or two questions, or answer all three. Go around the group on question 1 and let everyone share. Then go around again on question 2.

1. When you were a teenager, where did you most want to go?

- ☐ Anywhere but my hometown
- ☐ To LA or New York to become an actor
- ☐ Into the army to "see the world"
- ☐ Away from my parents
- ☐ To a romantic, exotic island
- ☐ Back in time to a more exciting era, like the Old West
- ☐ Hey, Disneyland would have been great for me!
- ☐ Into the world of my imagination
- ☐ Nowhere—I was always a homebody.

2. When in your life have you most felt like your life was going nowhere?

- ☐ As a teenager – I had no skills, no viable dreams, no life
- ☐ When I graduated and couldn't find a job
- ☐ When I was in a dead-end job
- ☐ When I reached middle age and realized I was no closer to my dreams
- ☐ When I retired and seemingly lost my purpose
- ☐ When my youngest child left home
- ☐ Right now
- ☐ I've never felt that way.
- ☐ other: ______________________________

3. What area of your life do you most feel is going nowhere right now?

- ☐ My professional life – I've definitely hit a plateau.
- ☐ My love life – "Where have all the flowers gone?"
- ☐ My spiritual life – I'm wandering in a wilderness.
- ☐ My family relationships – we all need to be re-introduced to each other.
- ☐ other: ______________________________

Bible Study

30-45 minutes

The Scripture for this week:

LEARNING FROM THE BIBLE

ISAIAH 49:1-7

1 Coastlands, listen to me;
distant peoples, pay attention.
The LORD called me before I was born
He named me while I was in my mother's womb.
2 He made my words like a sharp sword;
He hid me in the shadow of His hand;
He made me like a sharpened arrow,
He hid me in His quiver.
3 He said to me, "You are my servant, Israel;
I will be glorified in him."

BIBLE STUDY (cont'd)

[4]*But I myself said: I have labored in vain,*
I have spent my strength for nothing and futility;
yet my vindication is with the LORD,
and my reward is with my God.
[5]*And now, says the LORD,*
who formed me from the womb to be His servant,
to bring Jacob back to Him
so that Israel might be gathered to Him;
for I am honored in the sight of the LORD,
and my God is my strength –
[6]*He says,*
"It is not enough for you to be My servant
raising up the tribes of Jacob
and restoring the protected ones of Israel.
I will also make you a light for the nations,
To be My salvation to the ends of the earth."
[7]*That is what the LORD,*
the Redeemer of Israel, his Holy One says
to one who is despised,
to one abhorred by people,
to a servant of rulers:
"Kings will see and stand up,
and princes will bow down,
because of the LORD, who is faithful,
the Holy One of Israel – and He has chosen you."

...about today's session

A WORD FROM THE LEADER

Write your answers here.

1. What are three examples of how people can fail because the task they have defined for themselves is too small?

____

____

____

2. In what way was Israel "aiming too low"?

3. What Bible verse says to us that God wanted the nation of Israel to be a witness to other nations all along?

Identifying with the Story

In horseshoe groups of 6–8, explore questions as time allows.

1. When have you had the experience of "aiming too low" and not doing your best as a result?

2. In the work you have sought to do for God, when have you most felt you "labored in vain"? What made you feel that way?

3. In what way is God already using you to bless those beyond your own immediate family and community?

today's session

What is God teaching you from this story?

1. What goal did God give to the nation of Israel that can be seen as the goal of Christian servant leaders as well?

2. Why is being ethnocentric or parochial an insult to God?

TODAY'S SESSION (cont'd)

3. What three divisions of our witness did Jesus suggest at the beginning of the book of Acts?

____

____

____

4. What does it mean for a church to have its "lampstand" removed?

5. What happened to the nation of Israel around Isaiah's time when they just tried to look after "their own"?

Learning from the Story

In horseshoe groups of 6–8, choose an answer and explain why you chose what you did.

1. How would you have responded to God's larger task, had you been Isaiah?
   - ☐ "Yeah, me and who else?"
   - ☐ "Yes, but surely you don't mean nations like Iraq, Cuba, or Afghanistan!"
   - ☐ "I'm afraid my light is running out of batteries."
   - ☐ "Whatever you say!"
   - ☐ "Are you sure someone else might not be a better person to choose?"
   - ☐ other: _______________

2. What part of the larger family do you think you will have the hardest time serving in Christ's name?
   - ☐ People of a minority ethnic group
   - ☐ People who are really wealthy
   - ☐ People who are really poor
   - ☐ People from the big city
   - ☐ Homeless people
   - ☐ People who are from a country that is an enemy of ours
   - ☐ Democrats
   - ☐ Republicans
   - ☐ Small town people
   - ☐ Addicted people
   - ☐ other: __________

3. How does what has been discussed in this session make you feel about being "chosen" as a servant leader (v. 7)?

life change lessons

How can you apply this session to your life?

Write your answers here.

1. What are three things we can do to "expand our boundaries"?

   ____

   ____

   ____

2. What was the error of Jonah in regard to how he thought of God?

Caring Time

15-20 minutes

CARING TIME

Remain in horseshoe groups of 6-8.

This is the time to develop and express your caring for each other. Start by having group members respond to this question:

"What frustration from 'laboring in vain' would you like the group to pray for?"

Include these needs and concerns in your prayer, and then pray about the concerns on the Prayer/ Praise Report. Include prayer for the empty chair.

If you would like to pray silently, say "Amen" when you have finished your prayer, so that the next person will know when to start.

BIBLE STUDY NOTES

Reference Notes

Use these notes to gain further understanding of the text as you study on your own.

ISAIAH 49:2

my words like a sharp sword. Hebrews 4:12 tells us, "For the word of God is living and effective and sharper than any two-edged sword, penetrating as far as to divide soul, spirit, joints, and marrow." This tells us that the word of God can divide the almost indivisible ("soul" and "spirit") and can thus get to the heart of any matter. This was what Isaiah was saying that God was doing through him. Significantly, Revelation portrays the returning Christ as one with a sword coming from His mouth (Rev. 1:16; 2:12).

ISAIAH 49:3

I will be glorified in him. To fulfill their function as servant, Israel needed to glorify (focus praise and honor upon) God and not themselves. Israel failed in this mission and it was given to Christ whose followers became the new "Israel" (see Rom. 9:6-9).

ISAIAH 49:4

I have labored in vain. Israel as a nation repeatedly resisted God's leading and turned back to idolatry and injustice. This was extremely frustrating to the prophets who sometimes felt the people were forever "hearing, but never understanding" and "seeing, but never perceiving" (Isa. 6:9).

my vindication is with the LORD. In spite of his frustration, Isaiah realized that the true indication of one's success or failure is not how things look to people (including himself) but how God sees things. God had called him to this frustrating ministry (see again Isa. 6:9-13).

ISAIAH 49:5

to bring back Jacob to Him. Jacob was another name for Israel. Isaiah believed he had been called even before he was born to bring the rebellious nation of Israel back to God.

ISAIAH 49:6

a light for the nations. Here "nations" is another way of saying Gentile nations. While there were occasional Gentile converts to Judaism, not until Christ did this message fully find fulfillment. Christ Himself affirmed the faith of Gentiles (see Matt. 8:10-11), and the growth of the early church took off when it started reaching out to Gentiles (see for instance, Acts 10:9-48; 11:19-26; 15:3-4).

notes

notes

Session

13

A World to Gain

Prepare for the Session

	READINGS	REFLECTIVE QUESTIONS
Monday	Matthew 16:21-22	Do you try to protect your loved ones from all kinds of pain? How successful are you?
Tuesday	Matthew 16:23	Are you more concerned with human concerns or divine ones?
Wednesday	Matthew 16:24-26	What are you going after right now that you would sacrifice everything for? Is it worth it?
Thursday	Matthew 19:29	What have you had to leave behind to follow Christ? Have you done so with resentment or full confidence your sacrifice will be honored?
Friday	Matthew 13:44-45	What have you invested in the kingdom of God? Are you a confident investor or one who is hedging your bets?
Saturday	Matthew 6:19-21	Is your heart truly in the kingdom of God? Does the way you spend money show it?
Sunday	Matthew 6:33-34	How does your faith affect your feeling about what tomorrow will bring? Are you confident in the promises of God?

OUR GOALS FOR THIS SESSION ARE:

BIBLE STUDY

- To gain a greater appreciation of the rewards Christ holds out to those who follow Him as servant leaders
- To understand that self-fulfillment can only come from self-denial in Christ
- To appreciate the importance of following through on this study after this class has ended

LIFE CHANGE

- To review all the life change goals for previous lessons and target three for further work.
- To make a pact with at least one other member of this group to check up on each other in two weeks to see how well we are following through with life changes related to this course
- To focus your prayer this week on developing more of an attitude of self-giving

Icebreaker

10-15 minutes

GATHERING THE PEOPLE:

Form horseshoe groups of 6-8.

The "Futures" Market. Depending on time, choose one or two questions, or answer all three. Go around the group on question 1 and let everyone share. Then go around again on question 2.

1. When you were a teenager, which of the following predictions would your friends have made about your future?
   - ☐ "Most likely to succeed"
   - ☐ "Most likely to marry first"
   - ☐ "Most likely to spend some time in the slammer"
   - ☐ "Most likely to become famous"
   - ☐ "Most likely to run for office"
   - ☐ "Most likely to run an office"
   - ☐ "Most likely to just run"
   - ☐ "Most likely to be a stay-at-home mom"
   - ☐ "Most likely to be a stay-at-home dad"
   - ☐ "Future McDonald's Employee of the Month"

- ☐ "Future computer geek"
- ☐ "Future Miss America"
- ☐ other: ______________________________

2. What is the most significant thing you have experienced as an adult that nobody would have predicted for you when you were a teenager?

3. Complete this sentence: "The most exciting thing I see in my future right now is …"

Bible Study

30-45 minutes

The Scripture for this week:

LEARNING FROM THE BIBLE

MATTHEW 16:21-28

[21]From then on Jesus began to point out to His disciples that He
must go to Jerusalem and suffer many things from the elders, chief
priests, and scribes, be killed, and be raised the third day. [22]Then
Peter took Him aside and began to rebuke Him, "Oh no, Lord! This
will never happen to You!"
[23]But He turned and told Peter, "Get behind Me, Satan! You are
an offense to Me, because you're not thinking about God's concerns,
but man's."
[24]Then Jesus said to His disciples, "If anyone wants to come with
Me, he must deny himself, take up his cross, and follow Me. [25]For
whoever wants to save his life will lose it, but whoever loses his life
because of Me will find it. [26]What will it benefit a man if he gains the
whole world yet loses his life? Or what will a man give in exchange
for his life? [27]For the Son of Man is going to come with His angels in
the glory of His Father, and then He will reward each according to
what he has done. [28]I assure you: There are some of those standing
here who will not taste death until they see the Son of Man coming
in His kingdom."

...about today's session

A WORD FROM THE LEADER

Write your answers here.

1. What statement of Christ best expresses the irony of the Christian life?

2. What are three examples from life of how to receive something we first have to give?

 ____

 ____

 ____

3. How did Christ Himself exemplify the truth that to get life you first have to give it away?

Identifying with the Story

In horseshoe groups of 6–8, explore questions as time allows.

1. Who in your life has been the one to always try to keep bad things from happening to you?
   - ☐ My mom
   - ☐ My dad
   - ☐ An older brother or sister
   - ☐ My spouse
   - ☐ A grandparent
   - ☐ A best friend
   - ☐ other: ______________________________

2. When has someone tried to keep you from doing something risky when you felt it was something you really needed to do?

3. What is the closest you have come in your life to feeling like you had "sold out"— like what you had gained was at the cost of your "soul"?

today's session

What is God teaching you from this story?

1. What are two types of reward Christ promises us?

 ____

 ____

2. What famous person from the Middle Ages exemplifies finding life by giving it away?

3. How can self-fulfillment come from self-denial?

4. What New Testament passage connects our reward with a willingness to suffer with Christ?

5. What are two benefits of eternal life that Scripture seems to emphasize?

 ____

 ____

Learning from the Story

In horseshoe groups of 6–8, choose an answer and explain why you chose what you did.

1. What have you found yourself most willing to "sell your soul" for?
   - ☐ Material security
   - ☐ Those nice "toys" everyone else seems to have
   - ☐ The attention of the opposite sex
   - ☐ Power and prestige
   - ☐ The approval of friends
   - ☐ other: ______________________________

2. When have you felt like you may have unwittingly been used by Satan, as Peter was?

LEARNING FROM THE STORY (cont'd)

3. What is the next step you need to take to truly "deny yourself" and follow Christ?

   ☐ Spend more time listening to and supporting my family
   ☐ Find more ways to use my talents in service of people in need
   ☐ Find more ways to serve in the church
   ☐ Simply stop complaining so much about my own "woes"
   ☐ Spend less money on material things and more on helping others
   ☐ other: ____________________

life change lessons

How can you apply this session to your life?

Write your answers here.

1. Sustaining life changes requires what three things?

   ____

   ____

   ____

2. What Scripture encourages the spirit with which we should pray? Are there other similar Scriptures you know about which also point to this attitude?

Caring Time

15-20 minutes

CARING TIME

Remain in horseshoe groups of 6-8.

Pray for the concerns listed on the Prayer/Praise Report, then continue with the evaluation and covenant.

1. Take some time to evaluate the life of your group by using the statements below. Read the first sentence out loud and ask everyone to explain where they would put a dot between the two extremes. When you are finished, go back and give your group an overall grade in the categories of Group Building, Bible Study, and Mission.

GROUP BUILDING

On celebrating life and having fun together, we were more like a ...

wet blanket · **hot tub**

On becoming a caring community, we were more like a ...

prickly porcupine · **cuddly teddy bear**

BIBLE STUDY

On sharing our spiritual stories, we were more like a ...

shallow pond · **spring-fed lake**

On digging into Scripture, we were more like a ...

slow-moving snail · · · · · · · · · · · · · · · · · · · **voracious anteater**

MISSION

On inviting new people into our group, we were more like a ...

barbed-wire fence · · · · · · · · · · · · · · · · · · **wide-open door**

On stretching our vision for mission, we were more like an ...

ostrich · **eagle**

2. What are some specific areas in which you have grown in this course?

- ☐ understanding the true meaning of servant leadership
- ☐ better balancing my interests with the interests of others
- ☐ the importance of self-assurance to acting as a servant leader
- ☐ seeing how serving the most needy is the best way to serve God
- ☐ seeing how selfish ambition puts me in the place where God alone belongs in my life
- ☐ understanding the role of trust in being a good servant leader
- ☐ understanding that self-fulfillment can only come from self-denial in Christ
- ☐ other:______________________________

A covenant is a promise made to another in the presence of God. Its purpose is to indicate your intention to make yourselves available to one another for the fulfillment of the purposes you

CARING TIME (cont'd)

share in common. If your group is going to continue, in a spirit of prayer work your way through the following sentences, trying to reach an agreement on each statement pertaining to your ongoing life together. Write out your covenant like a contract, stating your purpose, goals, and the ground rules for your group.

1. The purpose of our group will be:

2. Our goals will be:

3. We will meet on __________________ (day of week).

4. We will meet for _____weeks, after which we will decide if we wish to continue as a group.

5. We will meet from ________ to ________ and we will strive to start on time and end on time.

6. We will meet at ______________________ (place) or we will rotate from house to house.

7. We will agree to the following ground rules for our group (check):

   - ☐ **PRIORITY:** While you are in this course of study, you give the group meetings priority.
   - ☐ **PARTICIPATION:** Everyone is encouraged to participate and no one dominates.
   - ☐ **RESPECT:** Everyone has the right to his or her own opinion, and all questions are encouraged and respected.
   - ☐ **CONFIDENTIALITY:** Anything said in the meeting is never repeated outside the meeting.
   - ☐ **LIFE CHANGE:** We will regularly assess our own life change goals and encourage one another in our pursuit of Christlikeness.
   - ☐ **EMPTY CHAIR:** The group stays open to reaching new people at every meeting.
   - ☐ **CARE and SUPPORT:** Permission is given to call upon each other at any time especially in times of crisis. The group will provide care for every member.
   - ☐ **ACCOUNTABILITY:** We agree to let the members of the group hold us accountable to the commitments which each of us make in whatever loving ways we decide upon.

- ☐ MISSION: We will do everything in our power to start a new group.
- ☐ MINISTRY: The group will encourage one another to volunteer and serve in a ministry, and to support missions by giving financially and/or personally serving.

Reference Notes

BIBLE STUDY NOTES

Use these notes to gain further understanding of the text as you study on your own.

MATTHEW 16:21 ***the elders, chief priests and scribes.*** These three groups made up the Sanhedrin, the official ruling body of the Jews.

MATTHEW 16:22 ***rebuke Him.*** Peter had just declared his faith that Jesus was the Messiah (16:16). However, he was startled by this teaching that went so much against his notion of who the Messiah was.

MATTHEW 16:23 ***Get behind me, Satan!*** By urging Jesus to back away from His teaching about suffering, Peter, like Satan, was tempting Jesus with the promise that He could have the whole world without pain or sacrifice (4:8-10).

MATTHEW 16:24 ***come with Me.*** To take on the role of a disciple, one committed to the teachings of a master.

deny himself. This means to regard one's personal ambitions as subservient to the kingdom of God.

take up his cross. This symbolized the grisly method of Roman execution, as the only people who bore crosses were prisoners on their way to their death. This would have startled the original hearers, as they thought the Messiah would overthrow Rome.

follow Me. This is a call for the disciples to imitate the lifestyle and embrace the values of their teacher.

MATTHEW 16:26 ***yet loses his life.*** All of us lose our lives in a physical sense, and so this means losing life's meaning and eternal promise. John said of Jesus, "In Him was life, and that life was the light of men." To lose Jesus is to lose your way in life. The list of people who seemed to have everything in the physical sense, but who in the end lost their way is exceedingly long: Elvis Presley, Marilyn Monroe, Jimi Hendrix, Janis Joplin, Kurt Cobain, John Belushi, Judy Garland. And that's just a sample of the people who are well-known.

MATTHEW 16:28 ***see the Son of Man coming.*** Jesus had already said that the kingdom of God was near (4:17; 10:23; 12:28). While some of this is a prediction of His second coming, it can also be seen as referring to either the transfiguration (17:1-13) or Christ's death and resurrection.

Group Directory

PASS THIS DIRECTORY AROUND AND HAVE YOUR GROUP MEMBERS FILL IN THEIR NAMES AND PHONE NUMBERS.

NAME	PHONE